The Edu

ISSUES
(formerly Issues for the Nineties)

Volume 35

Editor

Craig Donnellan

Independence
Educational Publishers
Cambridge

First published by Independence
PO Box 295
Cambridge CB1 3XP
England

British Library Cataloguing in Publication Data
The Education Crisis? – (Issues Series)
I. Donnellan, Craig II. Series
370.9'41

ISBN 1 86168 168 2

Printed in Great Britain
The Burlington Press
Cambridge

Typeset by
Claire Boyd

Cover
The illustration on the front cover is by
Pumpkin House.

CONTENTS

Chapter One: Educational Standards

Chapter Two: The Cost of an Education

Introduction

The Education Crisis? is the thirty-fifth volume in the **Issues** series. The aim of this series is to offer up-to-date information about important issues in our world.

The Education Crisis? looks at the standards and costs of education.

The information comes from a wide variety of sources and includes:
Government reports and statistics
Newspaper reports and features
Magazine articles and surveys
Literature from lobby groups
and charitable organisations.

It is hoped that, as you read about the many aspects of the issues explored in this book, you will critically evaluate the information presented. It is important that you decide whether you are being presented with facts or opinions. Does the writer give a biased or an unbiased report? If an opinion is being expressed, do you agree with the writer?

The Education Crisis? offers a useful starting-point for those who need convenient access to information about the many issues involved. However, it is only a starting-point. At the back of the book is a list of organisations which you may want to contact for further information.

*****

The National Curriculum

Curriculum aims and values

What is the National Curriculum for England?

The National Curriculum sets out a clear, full and statutory entitlement to learning for all pupils. It determines the content of what will be taught, and sets attainment targets for learning. It also determines how performance will be assessed and reported. An effective National Curriculum therefore gives teachers, pupils, parents, employers and their wider community a clear and shared understanding of the skills and knowledge that young people will gain at school. It allows schools to meet the individual learning needs of pupils and to develop a distinctive character and ethos rooted in their local communities. And it provides a framework within which all partners in education can support young people on the road to further learning.

This is also the first National Curriculum in England to include citizenship, from September 2002, as part of the statutory curriculum for secondary schools. Education in citizenship and democracy will provide coherence in the way in which all pupils are helped to develop a full understanding of their roles and responsibilities as citizens in a modern democracy. It will play an important role, alongside other aspects of the curriculum and school life, in helping pupils to deal with difficult moral and social questions that arise in their lives and in society. The handbooks also provide for the first time a national framework for the teaching of personal, social and health education. Both elements reflect the fact that education is also about helping pupils to develop the knowledge, skills and understanding they need to live confident, healthy, independent lives, as individuals, parents, workers and members of society.

Why have a National Curriculum?

The National Curriculum has four main purposes.

To establish an entitlement
The National Curriculum secures for all pupils, irrespective of social background, culture, race, gender, differences in ability and disabilities, an entitlement to a number of areas of learning and to develop knowledge, understanding, skills and attitudes necessary for their self-fulfilment and development as active and responsible citizens.

To establish standards
The National Curriculum makes expectations for learning and attainment explicit to pupils, parents, teachers, governors, employers and the public, and establishes national standards for the performance of all pupils in the subjects it includes. These standards can be used to set targets for improvement, measure progress towards those targets, and monitor and compare performance between individuals, groups and schools.

To promote continuity and coherence
The National Curriculum contributes to a coherent national framework that promotes curriculum continuity and is sufficiently flexible to ensure progression in pupils' learning. It facilitates the transition of pupils between schools and phases of education and provides a foundation for lifelong learning.

To promote public understanding
The National Curriculum increases public understanding of, and confidence in, the work of schools and in the learning and achievements resulting from compulsory education. It provides a common basis for discussion of educational issues among lay and professional groups, including pupils, parents, teachers, governors and employers.

About the school curriculum

Education influences and reflects the values of society, and the kind of society we want to be. It is important, therefore, to recognise a broad set of common values and purposes that underpin the school curriculum and the work of schools.

Foremost is a belief in education, at home and at school, as a route to the spiritual, moral, social, cultural, physical and mental development, and thus the well-being, of the individual. Education is also a route to equality of opportunity for all, a healthy and just democracy, a productive economy, and sustainable development. Education should reflect the enduring values that contribute to these ends. These include valuing ourselves, our families and other relationships, the wider groups to which we belong, the diversity in our society and the environment in which we live. Education should also reaffirm our commitment to the virtues of truth, justice, honesty, trust and a sense of duty.

At the same time, education must enable us to respond positively to the opportunities and challenges of the rapidly changing world in which we live and work. In particular, we need to be prepared to engage as individuals, parents, workers and citizens with economic, social and cultural change, including the continued globalisation of the economy and society, with new work and leisure patterns and with the rapid expansion of communication technologies.

Aims for the school curriculum

If schools are to respond effectively to these values and purposes, they need to work in collaboration with families and the local community, including church and voluntary groups, local agencies and business, in seeking to achieve two broad aims through the curriculum. These aims provide an essential context within which schools develop their own curriculum.

Aim 1: The school curriculum should aim to provide opportunities for all pupils to learn and to achieve.

The school curriculum should develop enjoyment of, and commitment to, learning as a means of encouraging and stimulating the best possible progress and the highest attainment for all pupils. It should build on pupils' strengths, interests and experiences and develop their confidence in their capacity to learn and work independently and collaboratively. It should equip them with the essential learning skills of literacy, numeracy, and information and communication technology, and promote an enquiring mind and capacity to think rationally.

The school curriculum should contribute to the development of pupils' sense of identity through knowledge and understanding of the spiritual, moral, social and cultural heritages of Britain's diverse society and of the local, national, European, Commonwealth and global dimensions of their lives. It should encourage pupils to appreciate human aspirations and achievements in aesthetic, scientific, technological and social fields, and prompt a personal response to a range of experiences and ideas.

By providing rich and varied contexts for pupils to acquire, develop and apply a broad range of knowledge, understanding and skills, the curriculum should enable pupils to think creatively and critically, to solve problems and to make a difference for the better. It should give them the opportunity to become creative, innovative, enterprising and capable of leadership to equip them for their future lives as workers and citizens. It should also develop their physical skills and encourage them to recognise the importance of pursuing a healthy lifestyle and keeping themselves and others safe.

Aim 2: The school curriculum should aim to promote pupils' spiritual, moral, social and cultural development and prepare all pupils for the opportunities, responsibilities and experiences of life.

The school curriculum should promote pupils' spiritual, moral, social and cultural development and, in particular, develop principles for distinguishing between right and wrong. It should develop their knowledge, understanding and appreciation of their own and different beliefs and cultures, and how these influence individuals and societies. The school curriculum should pass on enduring values, develop pupils' integrity and autonomy and help them to be responsible and caring citizens capable of contributing to the development of a just society. It should promote equal opportunities and enable pupils to challenge discrimination and stereotyping. It should develop their awareness and understanding of, and respect for, the environments in which they live, and secure their commitment to sustainable development at a personal, local, national and global level. It should also equip pupils as consumers to make informed judgements and independent decisions and to understand their responsibilities and rights.

The school curriculum should promote pupils' self-esteem and emotional well-being and help them to form and maintain worthwhile and satisfying relationships, based on respect for themselves and for others, at home, school, work and in the community. It should develop their ability to relate to others and work for the common good. It should enable pupils to respond positively to opportunities, challenges and responsibilities, to manage risk and to cope with change and adversity. It should prepare pupils for the next steps in their education, training and employment and equip them to make informed choices at school and throughout their lives, enabling them to appreciate the relevance of their achievements to life and society outside school, including leisure, community engagement and employment.

The interdependence of the two aims

These two aims reinforce each other. The personal development of pupils, spiritually, morally, socially and culturally, plays a significant part in their ability to learn and to achieve. Development in both areas is essential to raising standards of attainment for all pupils.

Educational outcomes

Today's younger generation is better educated than before. However, 22% of persons aged 18-24 have left the education system with only lower secondary education at best.

Younger generation is better qualified

Attainment levels of the population have improved significantly over the last thirty years. By comparing those currently leaving the education system with older generations, it is possible to monitor the trends over a long time-period. In 1997, 59% of persons aged 55-64 in EU-15 had completed only lower secondary education. This proportion had fallen to 32% among the younger age group 25-34. Greece, Spain, Italy and Portugal have the lowest levels of educational attainment but have witnessed the most significant increases in the last three decades. In these countries, the proportion of the youngest generation having completed at least upper secondary education is more than twice that of the oldest generation. As a result, the gap in attainment levels between the Member States is narrowing.

More than one in five 'school leavers' are low qualified

Although education levels continue to improve, up to 22% of 18-24-year-olds have left the education system without completing a qualification beyond lower secondary schooling (the equivalent of compulsory schooling in many cases).

To interpret this figure correctly, it is important to look at the activity status of 18-24-year-olds. EU-wide, 60% have left the education system and are either in employment, unemployed or inactive. The remaining 40% are still in education and it can be assumed that the majority will attain at least an upper secondary qualification (GCE 'A' levels, Baccalauréat, Abitur or equivalent) in the near future. The picture across the Union is far from homogeneous but divergences can largely be explained by the different proportions of young people still in education, e.g., countries such as Spain, Italy, Portugal and the United Kingdom with a relatively large share of low-qualified-18-24-year-olds also have a comparatively small proportion of young people still studying. In contrast, Germany and Denmark, with more than two-thirds of this age-group in education, have among the lowest share of low-qualified young people.

Higher qualifications tend to reduce the risk of unemployment . . .

In general, higher education qualifications seem to reduce, albeit to differing degrees, the chances of unemployment in all Member States. In EU-15, the unemployment rate of persons with a tertiary education qualification stood at 6% in 1997 compared with 10% for persons who had completed at best upper secondary education and 14% among those who had not gone beyond compulsory schooling.

. . . and increase earnings . . .

Data show also that earnings are more likely to be higher for better qualified people. In all Member States, full-time employees with tertiary education earn more on average than those who had completed upper secondary school. The difference is over 50% in Germany, France and Austria and 100% in Portugal. The earnings difference between those with upper secondary and those with lower secondary education was rather less (10-20%) in most countries and negligible in Greece, France, Ireland and Finland.

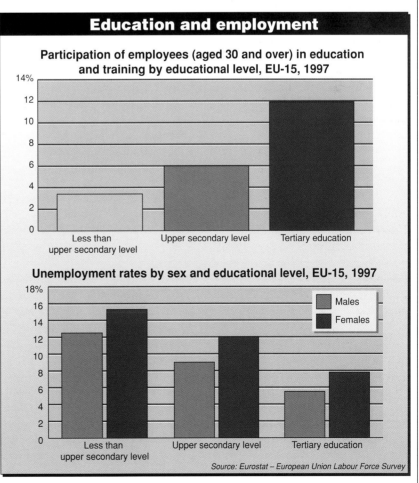

Education and employment

Participation of employees (aged 30 and over) in education and training by educational level, EU-15, 1997

Unemployment rates by sex and educational level, EU-15, 1997

Source: Eurostat – European Union Labour Force Survey

. . . and lead to more training opportunities at work

It is widely recognised that people in the labour force have to be equipped with the necessary skills to adapt in a labour market where the expectation of a 'job for life' has become increasingly outdated. Training of employees aged 30 and over is particularly prevalent in the Nordic countries, the Netherlands and the United Kingdom. For all countries, the higher the educational level of adults in employment, the greater the training opportunities afforded to them.

Methodological notes

Source: Eurostat – European Union Labour Force Survey (LFS) and Structure of Earnings Statistics.

The levels of education are defined according to ISCED (International Standard Classification of Education). Less than upper secondary corresponds to ISCED 0-2, upper secondary level to ISCED 3 and tertiary education to ISCED 5-7. The key indicator shows the number of persons aged 18-24 who have left the education system with low qualifications as a proportion of the total number of persons aged 18-24.

• The above information is an extract from *The social situation in the European Union 2000*, produced by the European Commission and Eurostat.

© *European Commission/EUROSTAT*

Jargon-busting guide

See the light with our jargon-busting guide to what some of those strange terms and initials actually mean

Baseline Assessment
An assessment of children's skills and abilities usually made by a teacher in the first weeks of starting school to help them plan lessons and measure progress. Areas covered include language, reading, maths and social skills.

DfEE
Department for Education and Employment.

EAZs
Education Action Zones. Groups of schools which receive £1 million a year for three to five years to raise standards and create new ideas.

Early Learning Goals
These set out the learning and development skills most children should have achieved by the end of the school reception year.

Early Years/Foundation Stage
Period of learning for children aged 3 to the end of the school reception year.

Exclusion
Exclusion means that children may not attend lessons or go on to the school premises for a set period of time, or permanently in the case of expulsion.

Independent Schools
Schools not funded by the state which get most of their finances from fees paid by parents. The largest ones are known as public schools.

INSET Days
In-service Education and Training. Inset days are set aside to allow teachers to update their skills and knowledge in order to raise pupil achievement.

KS (Key Stage)
Children's progress through school is measured in Key Stages. Key Stage 1 covers pupils from 5 to 7, Key Stage 2 from 7 to 11, Key Stage 3 from 11 to 14 and Key Stage 4 from 14 to 16.

LEA
Local Education Authority
A body responsible for providing education for pupils of school age in its area. It also has responsibility for early years, the youth service and adult education. An LEA is responsible for promoting high standards of education by ensuring that efficient primary and secondary education is provided. It also ensures that there are enough primary and secondary places with adequate facilities to meet the needs of pupils in the area.

National Curriculum
The basic framework setting out what children aged 5 to 16 in state schools should learn.

National Curriculum Levels
All pupils undergo national tests and teacher assessments at age 7,

11 and 14, commonly known as SATs. The school then sends a report telling parents what levels their child has reached.

Non-Contact Time
Teachers' work which does not involve teaching children in the classroom.

OFSTED
Office for Standards in Education. The body which inspects state-funded schools. OFSTED inspectors produce education reports to help improve standards.

Provider/Setting
Nursery and reception classes, playgroups, preschools, nurseries and accredited childminders in approved childminding networks are settings where early years education is provided.

School Performance Tables
Available towards the end of the year to help parents whose children are moving to secondary school choose where they want them to go. You can ask at school for a copy for your local area.

SEN
Special Educational Needs. Learning difficulties for which a child needs special help.

Specialist School
Schools who use government grants and business sponsorship to improve their facilities and resources in languages, art, sport or technology.

Study Support
Voluntary learning activities outside normal lessons to improve children's motivation and build their confidence.

Sure Start
A new strategy to improve services for children under four and their families in disadvantaged areas.

Teacher Assessment
A formal assessment made by a teacher when a child is 7, 11 and 14 to judge their progress.

• The above information is an extract from *Parent's Magazine* which is produced by the Department for Education and Employment and can be accesed on the internet at www.dfee.gov.uk/teacher/teachmag/

Britain bottom of literacy league

By John Clare, Education Editor

Half the adults in Britain have such poor levels of literacy and numeracy that they cannot cope with the demands of everyday life and work in a complex, advanced society, according to a study published yesterday.

Only four of the 29 countries belonging to the Organisation for Economic Co-operation and Development that took part in the survey had a lower average literacy score than Britain. They were Ireland, Hungary, Poland and Portugal. The most literate countries were Denmark, Finland, Germany, Holland, Norway and Sweden. In basic numeracy, only Ireland, Poland and Portugal scored lower than Britain.

The survey put Sweden top and Chile at the bottom in three literacy categories – prose, document and quantitative. Britain was ranked in the bottom half in each category. Based on tests administered to representative samples of adults aged 16 to 65 in each country, it divided literacy and numeracy skills into five levels.

Those scoring below level three could not say which of four film reviews was the least favourable; work out from a bicycle owner's manual how to ensure the seat was in the proper position; or convert a recipe for four servings into one for six. They were considered incapable of coping with the demands of everyday life and work. The proportion in Britain was 51 per cent.

Britain had the largest number of adults who watched television more than two hours a day – 60 per cent – of the 20 countries included in that part of the survey. The report said: 'Literacy scores are negatively

> ### Britain was alongside Ireland, the United States, and Australia in facing 'serious literacy problems for large proportions of their adult populations'

related to the amount of television people watch.' Britain came 13th in the table of adults who read a book at least once a month.

The report said: 'Countries differ markedly in the literacy of adult populations but none does so well that it has no literacy problems.' Britain was alongside Ireland, the United States, Switzerland, Canada and Australia in facing 'serious literacy problems for large proportions of their adult populations'.

• Nurses could be putting patients' lives at risk because poor standards in maths may lead to errors in calculating drug doses, it has been claimed. A meeting of the profession's regulatory body, the United Kingdom Central Council For Nursing, was told that maths was a general weakness in nursing students. Prof Bryn Davis, an ex-dean of a nursing school in Cardiff, said: 'In real-life drug decisions you are under pressure and it plays with your head.' Mr Davis said around six per cent of misconduct cases heard by the UKCC were linked to maladministration of drugs.

Tests show pupils have better grasp of basics

*By Liz Lightfoot,
Education Correspondent*

Children are getting a better grounding in the basics but their progress falters when they reach secondary schools, according to this year's national curriculum test results.

Improved scores for 11-year-olds in English and maths put the Government on track for reaching its 2002 target of three-quarters reaching the level expected for their age in maths and four-fifths in English. David Blunkett, the Education Secretary, who has pledged that he will resign if the targets are not met, said children had made 'tremendous progress'.

He admitted, however, that the one per cent drop in 14-year-olds reaching the required standard for English was disappointing. Some of the biggest improvements were in disadvantaged urban areas. Tower Hamlets, in east London, which has a high proportion of children speaking English as a second language, was the most improved local education authority.

The results of the 2000 tests sat by seven-, 11- and 14-year-olds last May also showed that children were much worse at writing than they were at reading. Boys had only slightly narrowed the gap with girls who outstripped them in both reading and writing. Standards of maths and English in primary schools continued to rise, but at a slightly lower rate than last year.

The percentage of 11-year-olds reaching the standard expected for their age – Level 4 – in English rose by four per cent to 75 per cent. Last year's increase was six per cent. In maths, 72 per cent reached the target, an increase of three per cent, compared with 10 per cent last year. Science results rose seven per cent, from 78 to 85 per cent of 11-year-olds reaching the required level.

> **'An additional 90,000 children achieved Level 4 in mathematics this year compared with 1998 and an extra 70,000 in English'**

Mr Blunkett attributed the improvement to hard work by teachers and pupils, but also to the introduction two years ago of the Government's literacy and numeracy strategies, aimed at reintroducing traditional teaching of the basics. He said: 'An additional 90,000 children achieved Level 4 in mathematics this year compared with 1998 and an extra 70,000 in English. The strategies are working because they focus on effective whole class teaching, on grammar, spelling and punctuation and on mental arithmetic.'

Science, for which there has been no national strategy, had improved because it had benefited from pupils' better maths and English skills, said Estelle Morris, the school standards minister. More detailed analysis of the results showed that poor writing was holding back pupils. Though 83 per cent of 11-year-olds passed the reading test, up five per cent on last year, only 55 per cent reached the standard for writing, a modest one per cent increase.

Mr Blunkett announced an extra £15 million for literacy and numeracy and published new guidance for schools on teaching writing. Grammar, spelling and punctuation needed to be improved, as did pupils' comprehension skills, said officials. Another disappointing aspect was the results of the English tests for

seven-year-olds, who have been taught according to the Government's strategies for two of their three years at school.

The percentage reaching Level 2, the expected level, was up by a modest one per cent in reading, writing and spelling, to 83, 84 and 72 per cent respectively. Maths, however, was up by three per cent to 90 per cent. Critics of the national literacy strategy accuse its authors of failing to understand the nature of traditional phonic teaching – the relationship between sounds and letters.

They say children should be taught to decode words from the start in a systematic way instead of learning to recognise them by sight, as they are still required to do under the strategy's mixture of methods. The strategy also teaches reading and writing separately unlike the phonic schemes, such as that used by Ruth Miskin, the head teacher of Kobi Nazrul, one of Tower Hamlets' most successful schools.

Results for 14-year-olds were better for maths and science. Sixty-five per cent reached the expected Key Stage 3 level in maths, up three

per cent on last year, and 59 per cent in science, a four per cent rise. There was a one per cent drop in English, however, from 64 to 63 per cent. The gap between boys and girls in English continued, though it narrowed among 11-year-olds to six per cent, from 15 per cent two years ago.

There was little difference between them in maths and science. The worst result for boys was in the English test for 14-year-olds where only 55 per cent reached the standard, compared with 72 per cent of girls.

The greater divide

Top freshers are again female and the gender gap is still growing, says Lee Elliot Major

The educational divide between the sexes continues to grow, with female students making up an ever larger share of the freshers entering university with the best A-level grades this year.

According to the latest official statistics for students enrolling last October, women accounted for 55% of degree entrants with As and Bs in their A-levels, and 56% of those with six or more Scottish Highers.

The figures confirm a steady trend over the last decade, reflecting the better performance of girls throughout the education system, from GCSE and A-level results to university graduation rates. A once male-dominated academic world has been transformed: women made up 54% of all degree applicants for the 2000 academic year.

It is particularly among the students with the highest A-level grades from state schools and further education colleges where girls outnumber boys. Nearly three out of five new degree students from the state sector with at least an A and two Bs in their A-levels were female this year.

This contrasts with the results at independent schools and grant maintained schools, which produce roughly equal numbers of girls and boys with top A-level grades.

Overall just under 26,000 female students enrolled with at least 26 A-level points, compared with just over 21,000 male students. Women accounted for 55% of top graded entrants in 2000, compared with 53.5% in 1999, and 51% in 1996, according to figures from the Universities and Colleges Admissions Service.

The figures confirm a steady trend over the last decade, reflecting the better performance of girls throughout the education system, from GCSE and A-level results to university graduation rates

---

The gaping educational gender divide is likely to cause further concerns for education ministers, who have already unveiled plans to recruit more male teachers in schools to provide role models for boys.

Other official statistics for universities show that women are less likely to drop out of degree courses than men, all other things being equal. Women also now make

up a larger proportion of graduates with upper seconds and firsts.

It may come as some comfort to ministers that the same educational trends are being experienced in the US and Ireland, however.

The gender split emerges as the clearest trend in an otherwise familiar set of enrolment figures. As with the previous year, under half of all university applicants came from the managerial and professional classes in 2000, with three-quarters of the 389,000 applicants being white and state schools again producing a quarter of all university applicants.

The academic institutions with the highest female enrolments reflect a preference among women students for the arts and social sciences.

At Goldsmiths College, 70% of new degree entrants were female, while a cluster of institutions attracted three out of five applications from women including Ulster, Middlesex, Glasgow Caledonian, Keele, Manchester Metropolitan and Bangor universities.

Institutions attracting less than two out of five applications from women were mainly those recognised for their strengths in science and technology and sport: Imperial College, London, Umist, Heriot-Watt and Loughborough.

The University of Bristol

emerges as the most popular university in the UK, receiving 35,000 applications – just over 12 for every place available. Other popular institutions included the London School of Economics (more than 11 applications for every place) and Warwick University (just under 10 applications for every place).

At the other end of the spectrum, the University of Central Lancashire and University of Wales, Lampeter, attracted fewer than three applications per place.

Cambridge is proving more popular – among men and women – than Oxford. Both universities had roughly 3,250 places available, but Cambridge received 12,000 applications, compared with only 9,700 attracted by Oxford. (Students are not allowed to apply to both universities.)

Cambridge's intake for 2000 was 48% women students – up 3% on the previous year. At Oxford, meanwhile, 46% of the undergraduate enrolments were female.

Bridging the gender gap

Can the government do anything but watch as the educational divide between the sexes grows wider each year? Lee Elliot Major considers the gender debate

By Lee Elliott-Major

It seems that there is now no stopping the advance of the educationally superior sex. Newly-released figures for last year's degree results show that women students for the first time outnumbered men in the total of firsts gained by university graduates. The results mark yet another educational milestone for females in what has been a year of academic triumphs over their male inferiors.

In a world where education is now a prerequisite for a half-decent job, the future omens for the male are not good. And the further you look back down the education chain, the grimmer it gets. Girls achieved a higher proportion of A-grades for the first time in last year's A-level results. The results for GCSEs showed that girls secured more top grades than boys across a greater number of subjects than ever before. And 25% more girls than boys achieved expected reading standards at age 11. In a decade's time, top male graduates could be an endangered species.

Can the government do anything but watch as the educational gender divide grows wider? Suggestions for improving the performance of boys come thick and fast: more male teachers, more vocational and craft based courses, a return to single-sex classrooms, schools and colleges, even allowing boys to start schooling at a later age than girls. But there is no easy solution. It is a complex cocktail of economic, social, cultural and genetic factors which appears to alienate males from schools, colleges and universities. Despite an inferior academic record overall, until now, men could always point to their domination of top-class degrees: this was the last bastion of male supremacy. Male students, it was argued, took more risks than their more steady, systematic female counterparts, producing the academic elite which made up for male shortcomings elsewhere. Every year the results appeared to bear out this stereotype. Men got more firsts. Women got more upper seconds.

But all that has now changed with the latest degree results. Just under 11,000 female students secured top-class degree honours in 2000 (almost 1,000 up on the 1999 figures), compared with 10,800 firsts for male graduates. Meanwhile, 67,500 females secured upper seconds compared with just over 42,000 males. This, remember, when males outnumber females in the population as a whole for this age group.

Some will point out that in proportional terms, men still secure more first-class degrees, and that the higher number of female firsts is an inevitable consequence of more women taking finals in the first place. But this ignores the unstoppable trend over recent years: females have been improving their academic grades throughout the education system for a decade. The results represent just one more breakthrough; many more are likely to come. Furthermore, despite their lower numbers, more male graduates secured the lowest degree grades.

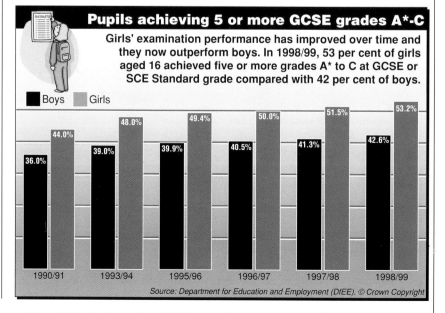

Pupils achieving 5 or more GCSE grades A*-C

Girls' examination performance has improved over time and they now outperform boys. In 1998/99, 53 per cent of girls aged 16 achieved five or more grades A* to C at GCSE or SCE Standard grade compared with 42 per cent of boys.

■ Boys ▨ Girls

Year	Boys	Girls
1990/91	36.0%	44.0%
1993/94	39.0%	48.0%
1995/96	39.9%	49.4%
1996/97	40.5%	50.0%
1997/98	41.3%	51.5%
1998/99	42.6%	53.2%

Source: Department for Education and Employment (DfEE). © Crown Copyright

The gender gap is by no means uniform. It widens and narrows for different academic disciplines and universities. A chasm emerges when girls are compared with boys from the poorest groups.

While they have made great strides in the maths and sciences in schools, girls have yet to overtake men in the numbers and results that they do in the arts, humanities and social sciences. University degree courses, in fact, increasingly reflect a gender split in academic preferences: few women for example opt for engineering and the physical sciences.

The signs are that it is particularly working-class males who are disenfranchised from the education system. Boys make up the majority of the 'lost generation' – the 150,000 or so 16-18-year-olds without any qualifications or official jobs. And the gender gap all but disappears in independent schools, and the most socially exclusive universities such as Cambridge and Oxford. Although it appears only a matter of time before the ivory towers of Oxbridge succumb to the rise of the female student: 48% of Cambridge enrolments last year were female, up 3% on the previous year.

So why are men turning away from education at a time when its economic and social worth cannot be overstated? One theory is that the educational underachievement is a symptom of a much more fundamental dilemma for the male race: a crisis in identity as traditional manufacturing jobs and family roles disappear. This feeling of hopelessness, it is argued, has already percolated through to even young boys. The international evidence substantiates this view: a widening gender gap is witnessed by other nations experiencing the same shift from manufacturing to service industries. In the US and Australia, concerns are now focusing on male anti-social and destructive behaviour, both inside and outside school: boys dominate the statistics for school suspensions and expulsions, suicides, road deaths, and delinquency.

Studies suggest that boys from very early on are under pressure to conform to a masculine stereotype – the macho, rebellious, unemotional male to whom study, school and authority are an anathema. Boys actively participate in their underachievement as part of the rejection of school. A recent UN study revealed the same phenomenon in many other countries. In the Caribbean, unlike the majority of the developing world, boys are doing significantly worse than girls at school. The reason? Schools were for 'sissies'. Is our education system failing to teach males in ways which better suit them? There are after all basic biological differences in the way females and males learn and communicate. Girls develop different skills at different rates, boys prefer to learn actively, rather than passively. Education ministers have vowed to recruit more male teachers in primary schools to provide role models for boys. They have also said that each school needs to develop its own individual strategy to tackle the underachievement of boys.

These small steps are to be welcomed. But it hardly amounts to the systematic response needed if the gaping educational divide is to be narrowed.

© Guardian Newspapers Limited 2001

How exams are fixed in favour of girls

Girls are doing better than boys in exams, but that does not mean that they are brighter, says Madsen Pirie. What has happened is that exams have been feminised – and so has the country

Female examinees continue to carry all before them. First, they made waves in the GCSE exams, outperforming their male counterparts in every year since GCSEs replaced O-levels in 1988. Then, last summer, and for the first time, they edged ahead of boys in A-level results, with girls gaining more A-grade passes than boys did. Now they are reported to have completed the hat-trick, winning more university degrees with first-class honours than boys could manage.

According to the Higher Education Statistics Authority, more than 11,000 women gained first-class honours degrees at Britain's 170 universities, against only 10,800 achieved by the men. This reverses

The number of women with firsts has trebled in a decade, with women now leading the field in 12 of the 17 subject areas, including medicine

the previous year's position, when 10,500 men gained firsts, as opposed to 10,200 women. Only five years ago, men gained 1,800 more first-class honours degrees than women. The number of women with firsts has trebled in a decade, with women now leading the field in 12 of the 17 subject areas, including medicine, law and business. Partly, they gain more of the firsts because there are more of them. They make up 55 per cent of the university population, and gain more of all qualifications. There is, nonetheless, a clear trend running through education.

Analysts have been quick to assign causes. The superior performance of girls at GCSEs represented, we were told, the fact that girls mature much earlier, and take a more serious-minded, adult attitude to education. Last year's A-level results gave the commentators a field-day. Educational psychologists solemnly laid blame on the 'laddish' culture espoused by schoolboys. It was 'uncool', we were told, for boys to be seen as swots. Even the ones who did work had to do so furtively for fear of losing face with their peer-group. Some commentators even managed to lay the blame on black teenagers, for setting poor role-models for their white, middle-class counterparts, and giving academic success no street cred. David Blunkett's office set up an inquiry headed by Judith Ireson of the University of London's Institute of Education. Part of its remit has been to investigate whether the 'slump' in boys' results has been caused by the rise of laddishness.

As for the success of girls at university, there has been no shortage of explanations. Tony Higgins, of the University Admissions Service, says that 30 years of work encouraging girls to stay in higher education has paid dividends. No doubt others will tell us earnestly that male under-graduates prefer to indulge in the drinking and clubbing culture of university life, while their more serious-minded female colleagues are hitting the books until the library closes. Some might see the extra effort by women as a result of the changing nature of society. Few women now think in terms of marriage as a career; most assume they will have to work for a living, and that qualifications will matter more than they did before. A recent MORI poll for the Adam Smith Institute showed that 48 per cent of women, marginally more than men, list 'owning and running my own business' among their career aspirations. If women once viewed university qualifications less seriously, it is no longer true.

There is an alternative explanation for the recent successes of girls, which many of those involved in education accept readily. It is that

boys and girls have not changed very much in their habits and skills, but the examinations themselves have changed. The old exams — O-levels, A-levels and degree finals — tended to reward the qualities which boys are good at. That is, they favoured risk-taking and grasp of the big picture, rather than the more systematic, consistent, attention-to-detail qualities which favour girls. The old O-level, with its high-risk, swot-it-all-up-for-the-final-throw, and then attempt not more than four out of nine questions, was a boys' exam. The GCSE which replaced it places much more emphasis on systematic preparation in modules, worked on consistently over time. It is not surprising that girls have done better since the change was made, since GCSEs represent the way girls work.

It is not that one approach is better than the other, just that they are different. One brings out the strengths of boys, the other brings out the strengths of girls. Girls began to do better, not because the boys 'slumped', but because the exams were feminised. A Cambridge don neatly encapsulated the difference to me: 'The boy sees the big picture,

takes risks, and often misses important material. The girl is systematic, does the detailed work, and sometimes misses the central thesis.' He gave a vivid account of a recent oral, in which a boy and a girl were both defending their dissertation for finals. 'They went to type,' he said. 'The girl had done an amazing amount of detail, but had not grasped what it all added up to. The boy saw instantly what it was all about, but was fuzzy on the supporting evidence. Both of them gained firsts.'

IQ tests routinely recognise the difference, and make allowances accordingly. Boys score better with numbers, pattern recognition, and abstract reasoning. Girls do better with language and situational logic. An IQ test intended for both sexes will have sections which play to each of the different skills, to avoid being easier for the one sex than for the other. Mensa, the high-IQ society, uses a variety of different tests, and its educational psychologists take it as axiomatic that girls do better on some, boys on others.

Chris Woodhead, the government's former chief inspector of schools, recognises the change. 'There is no doubt,' he says, 'that elements have been incorporated into school examinations which girls find easier to do than boys.'

Professor Alan Smithers, of Liverpool University's Centre for Education and Employment Research, takes a broader view. 'Exams are simply easier,' he says. 'They present less of a challenge, and are more easily coped with by conscientious and consistent application. Girls apply themselves more.' Not only does he think that GCSEs are less challenging than O-levels because they cater for a wider ability range; he also points out that A-levels have been broadened, incorporating modules (optional components) and covering a greater range of subjects. Twice as many people are now expected to pass through university as were once expected to pass the 11-plus. 'Where once there was history and physics,' he says, 'we now have health studies, social care, leisure and tourism.'

Professor Smithers also thinks that the changes in assessment are significant. He points out that what used to be decided by terminal examination is often now determined in part by modules and continuous assessment, both of which favour the more systematic approach taken by girls rather than the high-risk strategy which appeals more to boys.

Even the method of marking has changed. Claire Fox, director of the Institute of Ideas and a former teacher, says that markers formerly used their professional expertise on a loose set of criteria to see which grade a script merited, or whether it should fail. Today, a more prescriptive and detailed checklist is issued, including such factors as 'situated in historical context', 'personal response to the literature', or 'shows awareness of style'. This can result, she claims, 'in rewarding blindly those who methodically — even dully — fulfil the checklist criteria, regardless of passion, insight or flair, and penalising those of a more creative or individual style'.

Mark Coote, a teacher at the City of London Freemen's School at Ashtead, thinks that 'the whole nature of the GCSE and AS/A-level examinations favours the girls' approach to working'. His 17 years of teaching experience has persuaded him that girls fare better over modular courses where they can plan their study time and strategy, and that they are better timekeepers, and have the self-discipline to meet deadlines. 'Boys,' he says, 'do play a high-risk strategy, preferring last-minute cramming. They tend to rise to the challenge of final examinations where there is all (or nothing) to play for.' He cannot, in his teaching experience, remember a single girl pupil who has missed a coursework deadline for GCSE assessment, other than through genuine illness. He has, however, 'lost count of the number of boys who have worked until three in the morning to meet the deadline, or missed it altogether. Boys perform less well in coursework than girls,' he tells us, 'although they make up ground in the final exams.'

The questions themselves have changed. An O-level question was demanding of fact and understanding. Candidates might have been asked to outline the main arguments presented in the 1689 Bill of Rights and the Act of Settlement of 1701, and the effect this might have had on Catholics. A modern GCSE question, encouraging empathy, might ask, 'How might you have felt as a Jewish child growing up in Nazi Germany?' An old O-level question might have asked why the Jacobite Rebellions of 1715 and 1745 ended in failure. A typical GCSE question on the same subject, using stimulus material such as a picture, might ask as its first question (carrying one mark), 'Why is Bonnie Prince Charlie wearing tartan?'

It is not that the exams were right before, and are wrong now. It is that they were boy-friendly before, and are now girl-friendly

---

Given these facts, the outcome is less surprising. If we change the structure of our examinations, and the methods by which they are marked, in ways which play to girls' strengths, we can hardly be surprised if boys do less well than they did before. It is not that boys are becoming less able or less academic than they were previously. It is that they now face examinations which have been feminised, and which fail to bring out their strong points. It is not that the exams were right before, and are wrong now. It is that they were boy-friendly before, and are now girl-friendly. The previous exams discriminated against girls just as much as the present ones discriminate against boys. Commentators have observed that modern society has become to some degree feminised. The same has happened to examinations. They have been remade, perhaps unconsciously, in a feminine image which downplays competition and risk, both of which favour boys.

If we wish boys to do better in GCSEs, A-levels and university degrees, we do not need psychological insights into the 'laddish' culture, or to provide them with more worthy role-models, or to tell them that they are underachievers. We need examinations which appeal to them and which bring out their strengths. One answer might be to have different examination boards providing different styles of exam, so that teachers or students could select ones which suited the character of the applicant. Girls might be entered for those which featured more modules and coursework; boys might be steered towards ones in which the final examination counted for more.

Ultimately, we have to ask ourselves what sort of society we are producing if we feminise the entry qualification into its leadership positions. If we select the methodical over the risk-takers, male or female, and the systematic in preference to those with insight, will Britain still be capable of meeting the challenges the world throws its way? While the country might be more peaceable, more sensitive to the needs of its citizens, and more efficient in applying itself to the detail of good management, we might ask if it will still be as inventive and creative? Will it still produce penicillin and hovercraft? Or will it just produce civil servants?

One might wonder how the British economy would fare if its educational system had extinguished the flash and fire of entrepreneurial zeal, and replaced it with the duller expectations of systematic and steady progress. One might also wonder, in times of rapid change, if such a Britain would be adaptive, capable of responding instantly when needs arose? The old examinations were as much a test of character as of educational attainment. They tested the ability to stand up under pressure, and to hold one's nerve in a crisis. The new exams undoubtedly test character, too, but of a very different quality. Whether we like it or not, they are helping to determine the sort of country we will become.

• Dr Madsen Pirie is president of the Adam Smith Institute.

© 2001 The Spectator

Educational inequality

Ethnic groups not benefiting equally from rising standards, says report

A new review of research into inequalities of educational attainment among different ethnic groups warns that schools and LEAs need help to develop policies leading to equality and inclusion.

Educational Inequality: Mapping Race, Class and Gender offers a synthesis of research evidence to analyse the factors contributing to differing achievements of the major ethnic groups in England. It is the work of David Gillborn of the University of London, Institute of Education and Heidi Safia Mirza of Middlesex University. It is published by the Office for Standards in Education.

The report notes that all ethnic groups have shared in the national rise in standards demonstrated by the percentage of pupils with five or more higher grade GCSE passes, but their rise has not been equal.

Indian pupils have made the greatest gains, according to data from the Youth Cohort Surveys of 1988, 1995 and 1997, enabling them to overtake their white peers as a group. Bangladeshi pupils have also improved significantly, but not enough to close the gap on white youngsters.

African-Caribbean and Pakistani pupils have drawn least benefit from the rising levels of attainment: the gap between them and their white peers is larger now than a decade ago.

The review uses for the first time data submitted by local education authorities (LEAs) to the Department for Education and Employment in support of applications for Ethnic Minority Achievement Grant (EMAG).

The researchers urge caution in interpreting the data from LEA bids for EMAG because of the inconsistency with which applications were made. Almost a third of the 118 LEAs bidding for grants, for example, did not record current GCSE attainment by ethnic origin.

Indeed, the EMAG submissions show that ethnic monitoring is still not a universal feature of LEA data gathering. They nevertheless offer a unique glimpse of the variation in minority attainment between localities.

Indian pupils have made the greatest gains, according to data from the Youth Cohort Surveys, enabling them to overtake their white peers as a group

---

Of just six authorities who included baseline assessments by ethnic group in their submissions, one large urban authority showed that African-Caribbean pupils enter compulsory schooling as the highest achieving group but leave as the group least likely to gain five high grade GCSEs. Data from this LEA show that the relative attainment of African-Caribbean pupils declines at each key stage. 'That any ethnic group could enter school 20 percentage points in advance of the average but leave 21 points behind, opens up an important area for educational debate on ethnic minority attainment,' say the researchers.

The report says that data gathered through baseline assessments is a potentially vital area worthy of rigorous analysis. 'By failing to collect baseline data by ethnicity, the DfEE and individual LEAs may be seeing only half the picture. Based on an examination of LEA target setting the report also reveals that there is no clarity about planning for an inclusive standards agenda. Some LEAs' plans actually anticipate greater inequalities in the future,' they say.

© OFSTED (Office for Standards in Education). Crown Copyright 2000

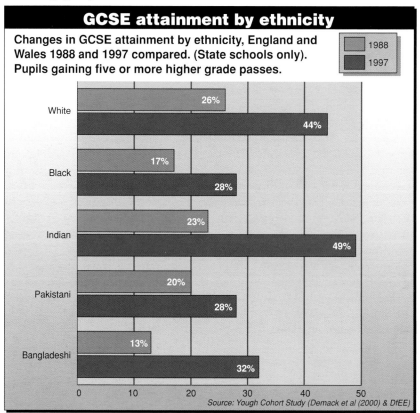

GCSE attainment by ethnicity

Changes in GCSE attainment by ethnicity, England and Wales 1988 and 1997 compared. (State schools only). Pupils gaining five or more higher grade passes.

- 1988
- 1997

White: 26% (1988), 44% (1997)
Black: 17% (1988), 28% (1997)
Indian: 23% (1988), 49% (1997)
Pakistani: 20% (1988), 28% (1997)
Bangladeshi: 13% (1988), 32% (1997)

Source: Yough Cohort Study (Demack et al (2000) & DfEE)

Black pupils three times more likely to be barred

By Liz Lightfoot,
Education Correspondent

Fears that some teachers treat black children more harshly than white have been confirmed by inspectors. Not only are black pupils up to three times more likely to be expelled, they tend to receive longer short-term exclusions.

A report by Ofsted, published yesterday, said that inspectors found evidence that black children were excluded for five days and white pupils for three for the same or similar incidents. It said: 'In some schools the length of fixed period exclusions received by black and white pupils is different. Few schools appear to have developed the confidence to discuss such issues straightforwardly.'

Mike Tomlinson, the Chief Inspector of Schools, launching the report, said: 'While it does not follow that schools treated pupils differently because of their ethnicity, they certainly could leave both pupils and parents with the impression that they had done so.'

The study of truancy and behaviour was requested by David Blunkett, the Education Secretary, and it looked at 10 urban secondary schools with high levels of truancy and exclusion. The report was also based on short visits to a further 80 secondaries and evidence from visits and inspections of local education authorities.

It found that black Caribbean boys were most likely to be permanently excluded, followed by other black pupils. They were also more frequently excluded for short periods for what schools called 'challenging behaviour'. Mr Tomlinson said that the schools had not realised that they were treating pupils differently until they analysed the data. There was a reluctance to address the highly-charged issue of race.

He drew back from blaming racism for the inconsistent sanctions, saying that the evidence did not allow Ofsted to draw any conclusions about why it happened. 'It could be part or all of the reasons, or there could be other reasons. What we have done is no more than open the box. A great deal more work needs to be done to understand what is happening.'

> *In some schools the length of fixed period exclusions received by black and white pupils is different. Few schools appear to have developed the confidence to discuss such issues straightforwardly*

Inconsistent approaches to discipline had led to confusion in some schools which did not clearly explain the behaviour that was considered unacceptable and the punishment imposed for it. The same incident might, for example, be recorded as 'swearing' in one instance and 'challenging behaviour' in another.

Some teachers found the 'self-confidence, apparent or otherwise' of some black Caribbean boys particularly intimidating, says the report. There was also, in some schools, a reluctance to discipline them for minor misdemeanours for fear of accusations of racism. Misbehaviour increased until exclusion followed.

Schools needed to analyse their reports of poor behaviour and punishments and if ethnic minority children appeared to be more harshly treated the reasons had to be explored, said Mr Tomlinson. He reported that bullying continued to be a problem, much of it surreptitious and unreported. Evidence suggested that girls were more involved in sustained bullying than boys, though less likely to use violence.

Mr Tomlinson said: 'Bullying among girls is centred around dress, personal characteristics and looks. There are a whole raft of things which can bear down on girls and have a dramatic influence on their confidence and motivation to do well at school.' There was evidence that girls and boys were bullied for doing well in their studies. 'Being bullied because they are doing well forces some young people to decide they won't work so hard because it will remove the cause of the unpleasantness.'

Overall, the message from the study was that good teaching provided the best incentive for both good behaviour and attendance. Casual attitudes on the part of parents towards their children's truancy were also a factor. Prof Tony Sewell, an expert in race and education at Leeds University, said he was not surprised at the findings. 'The biggest barrier is the widespread refusal of teachers to speak about race, often because they are scared it could bring down the racial equilibrium in the school.

'Ofsted, too, seems unwilling to tackle issues behind the exclusions, but it can't be hypocritical. It must help schools by saying it expects them to talk about race issues and will look at them during routine inspections.'

The Commission for Racial Equality said it had issued guidance on avoiding discrimination in exclusions three years ago. The Department for Education said the exclusion of black pupils was falling twice as fast as those of others. There had been a 32 per cent fall in the exclusion rate of black pupils since 1997, compared with 16 per cent for other children.

© Telegraph Group Limited, London 2000

Worsening behaviour 'linked to teacher shortage'

Ofsted says rise in use of supply staff is contributing to poor attitudes among secondary school pupils

By Will Woodward, Education Editor

Staff shortages are contributing to worse behaviour by pupils, lack of academic progress from ages 11-14, and a widening gap between low and high performers at secondary level, the chief inspector of schools in England warned yesterday.

Delivering his first annual report, Mike Tomlinson said there was 'much to celebrate', particularly in primary schools where in 40% of those inspected there was no unsatisfactory teaching at all. 'The great majority of parents are pleased with their children's education,' he said.

The proportion of poor teaching has fallen from one lesson in five in 1995 to one in 20 now, and the proportion of good or better teaching has risen from 40% to 60% over the same period. In primary schools, the improvement was greatest in the most disadvantaged areas.

But as the differences between the best and worst-performing primary schools reduced, the gap was widening among secondary schools. Secondary schools serving the most disadvantaged pupils had improved their results but the biggest gains were made by schools already performing well.

The chief inspector said there was a 'clear link' between inadequate staffing and underachievement. Schools in poorer areas were also much more likely to have temporary teachers.

> **'There is growing evidence of the adverse impact of high staff turnover, widespread use of temporary teachers and a poor match between teachers' qualifications and the subjects taught'**

'Urgent action is more than ever needed on the recruitment and retention of teachers, as the government plainly acknowledges,' Mr Tomlinson said. 'The very real progress made by schools in recent years in raising standards is at risk unless current trends are reversed and gaps are filled with well-qualified specialists.

'There is growing evidence of the adverse impact of high staff turnover, widespread use of temporary teachers and a poor match between teachers' qualifications and the subjects taught.'

There were shortages not only in subjects such as technology, foreign languages and maths, but also religious education, music and, in some London schools, even English.

Mr Tomlinson's verdict was welcomed by the teaching unions but was a blow to ministers, who have spent the past few months playing down union talk of crisis-level teacher shortages.

Tony Blair and David Blunkett will next week launch a green paper on the secondary sector which they have identified as the key education challenge in their second term.

For the first time in recent years, inspectors reported an increase in poor behaviour at secondary schools. One secondary school in 12 had unsatisfactory behaviour.

A small minority of pupils had behaviour and attitudes which challenged even the best teachers,

the report said. But inspectors also recorded inconsistent behaviour by some pupils. 'You can go from one class to the next and watch behaviour turn from angelic to devilish within 35 minutes,' said Ofsted's head of inspection, David Taylor. Teacher unions blamed a reduction in the number of pupils excluded after a government initiative.

The report said that too many pupils fail to make good progress in the early years of secondary school. 'Although pupils generally begin their secondary education enthusiastically in year seven, there is a tendency for commitment and motivation to fall away in years eight and nine,' Mr Tomlinson said. He added that schools were not doing enough to support the transition from primary level.

Ofsted linked the problems to the increased use of supply staff and temporary teachers. 'I think it is hardly surprising that in these circumstances pupils, in a sense, decide this is not for them and vote with their feet in one way, shape or form,' Mr Tomlinson said. Mr Taylor said that in schools with shortages, permanent staff concentrated on GCSE classes at the expense of the 11-14s.

Mr Tomlinson released a list of 281 'successful' schools, who have had good inspection reports and performed well in national tests given the circumstances of their schools. Some 226 formerly failing schools were removed from special measures in the period covered by the report, the academic year 1999-2000. Inspectors visited 4,700 schools, about one-sixth of those in England.

Mr Tomlinson echoed many of the themes of his predecessor, Chris Woodhead, whom he replaced in December. He repeated complaints about funding disparities which Mr Tomlinson said varied at primary school between £1,400 and £2,600 per pupil and at secondary between £1,700 and £3,000. The relative poor performance of boys showed no sign of changing – 'something of a national scandal,' said Mr Taylor.

Estelle Morris, the school standards minister, welcomed the report, and congratulated teachers but said: 'The extent of improvement is still too variable, especially in secondary schools, and this will be an important challenge in the coming years.' She added that the government was spending £174m on tackling bad behaviour – 10 times more than the last Tory government.

John Dunford, of the Secondary Heads' Association, spoke for most in welcoming 'the balanced account of the state of our education service'. Doug McAvoy, general secretary of the National Union of Teachers, said: 'Ofsted's warnings about the effects of teacher shortages echo the NUT's own warnings and should cause the government to end its complacency.'

But Theresa May, the shadow education secretary, said the fact that standards had risen was down to the dedication of teachers across the country rather than the government. '[The government] has done everything it can to hinder heads and teachers with centralised diktats, pointless initiatives and mountains of time-consuming bureaucracy,' she said.

Statistics

- In schools where 5% or fewer pupils take free school meals, temporary teachers account for 3% of staff
- In schools where 50% of pupils take free school meals, temporary teachers account for 10% of staff
- Seven out of eight secondary schools are effective, as are nine out of 10 primary schools
- More than six out of 10 lessons in both primary and secondary schools are well taught
- Behaviour is unsatisfactory in one in 50 primary but in one in 12 secondary schools

© Guardian Newspapers Limited 2001

Truancy checks in city centre cut youth crime

By Liz Lightfoot, Education Correspondent

Truancy checks in York city centre have cut youth crime by two-thirds, says the Department for Education.

The truancy watch schemes were introduced a year ago and all children, even those with an adult, are questioned if seen on the streets during school hours. Jacqui Smith, the schools minister, praised the scheme for reducing youth crime by 67 per cent, as she announced an extra £43 million to tackle truancy.

She said the amount of money available for sweeps and other such initiatives, £174 million, was 10 times that available when Labour came to power. She said: 'Too many children are missing school and cutting their chances of success in life. Some schools are raising attendance levels, but more needs to be done to reduce significantly the 50,000 pupils away from school without permission on any given day.'

The money will fund more truancy sweeps in which police and education welfare officers pick up youngsters. It will also pay for schemes to make parents and the community more aware of truancy and to fund mentors for disaffected pupils.

The Education Department said telephoning parents whose children were absent had more than halved unauthorised absences at Valentines High School in Ilford, east London. Money from the Government had funded staff to make the calls. Attendance rates had been improved by five per cent where vocational taster courses and work experience programmes had been introduced.

Support from shopkeepers who alerted Montgomery High School, in Blackpool, to suspected truants had helped it to achieve attendance of 100 per cent.

© Telegraph Group Limited, London 2001

Teacher shortages threaten standards

By John Clare

There has been a 'really quite tremendous' improvement in teaching quality and primary and secondary school standards over the past five years, Mike Tomlinson, the new head of Ofsted, said yesterday.

It was a cause for celebration that only one lesson in 20 was now unsatisfactory, most parents were pleased with their children's education and primary schools were doing better than ever. However, Mr Tomlinson, who was presenting Ofsted's annual report for the last year that Chris Woodhead, his predecessor, was in office, warned the Government that all the gains made were now at risk.

A shortage of good secondary school teachers, particularly in maths, science, modern foreign languages, design and technology and even English was already having an adverse impact. 'Most vacancies are eventually filled but heads report that there are few good applicants and sometimes few applicants at all, in an increasing range of subjects,' the report said.

As a result, subjects were being taught by non-specialists, use of temporary teachers was widespread and high staff absence and turnover were leading to serious disruption.

One consequence was that, for the first time in many years, inspectors reported increasing levels of bad behaviour, which was the response of pupils to poor teaching.

Action to improve the recruitment and retention of teachers was more urgent than ever, he said.

A shortage of good secondary school teachers, particularly in maths, science, modern foreign languages, design and technology and even English is already having an adverse impact

Another problem for the Government was that, despite the extra billions it said it was putting into education, one secondary school in four – 850 in all – did not have enough money for books and equipment. Nor did one primary school in 15 – another 1,200 schools.

Such a shortage of resources was affecting the quality of education and the situation was exacerbated by the 'unfair' way schools were funded. While some primary schools received £2,600 a year per pupil, others had to manage with £1,400. Some secondary schools received £3,000 a pupil but others had to make do with £1,700.

'Given that all schools have to teach the same statutory national curriculum, these variations are difficult to understand and quite unacceptable,' he said. 'It's time someone decided how much money schools need to do their job.'

Similarly impervious to lavish Government funding was schools' teaching of information and communications technology. Although it has absorbed more than £1 billion, it was by far the worst taught subject at primary and secondary level.

The report attributed much of the significant improvement in primary education to the national literacy and numeracy strategies. They had led to higher attainment, an emphasis on whole-class teaching, clearer learning objectives and good choice of subject content.

However, there was no place for complacency. One primary school

in 10 – nearly 2,000 schools – was 'ineffective'. Leadership by the head was weak, there were high levels of unsatisfactory teaching and substantial underachievement by the children.

Across all primary schools, the main weakness was in teaching pupils, especially boys, how to write. Although writing was an essential skill, more than a half of boys and a third of girls failed to reach the expected standard at 11. They could not compose text that conveyed clear meaning.

Teachers failed to teach writing systematically and did not pay enough attention to grammar, not least because they did not know enough about it themselves. Improvement in secondary schools had been more gradual but the quality of teaching was now judged good in six lessons out of 10. The greatest weaknesses were in the first three years.

Although pupils generally began their secondary education enthusiastically in Year 7, motivation and behaviour tended to fall away in Years 8 and 9. The pace of learning slowed, many children simply marked time and, on average, one out of the three years was wasted.

By the end of Key Stage 3 when pupils are 14, a third failed to reach the expected level in literacy or numeracy. This was also the time when bad behaviour surfaced.

The proportion of ineffective secondary schools was one in eight – 450 schools mostly serving disadvantaged areas – and the gap between advantaged and disadvantaged schools was widening.

Also widening, and showing no signs of narrowing, was the gap in achievement between boys and girls, described by David Taylor, director of inspections, as a 'national scandal'. Girls were doing better than boys in every subject at GCSE and A-level.

Estelle Morris, the schools minister, admitted that there were 'still important challenges' for schools.

NUT tells Government how to end teacher shortage crisis

Information from the National Union of Teachers (NUT)

The National Union of Teachers has set out a five-point plan to overcome teacher shortages in a letter to Estelle Morris, Schools Minister, from Doug McAvoy, NUT General Secretary.

The Union's Executive has called for an urgent meeting with the Minister to discuss its proposals in an attempt to reassure teachers and prevent more schools being forced on to a four-day week. It has repeated its warning that it is determined to protect its 202,000 in-service members from excessive burdens arising from the shortages. It calls for:

1. A 12.5 per cent or £2,000 pay increase, whichever is the greater, across the board with a pledge to bring teachers' pay into line with other professions recruiting graduates;
2. Additional funding to schools to improve levels of back-up staff releasing teachers from administrative tasks to concentrate on teaching;
3. Limits on all class sizes and working hours, guaranteed marking and preparation time, and financial support to schools and teachers to ensure access to professional development;
4. Support from national and local government for schools facing unacceptable pupil behaviour and acceptance that schools may exclude pupils who exhibit such behaviour; and
5. Continued commitment from the Government to, and expansion of, improvements in school buildings and the provision of ICT equipment and training.

General Secretary Doug McAvoy said, 'The Government has to convince existing teachers that it is serious about overcoming this crisis. If they are to be persuaded, the Government must, first and foremost, admit the full extent of the problem and stop hiding behind fictitious official vacancy levels.

'Schools have gone to extraordinary and sometimes inappropriate lengths to cope as Alan Smithers' report for the Union showed clearly. The Government must admit the extent of that cover-up rather than insisting that shortages are a problem in London and the south-east in a handful of schools only.

'Once it stops going into denial and instead seeks agreement on solutions, teachers, young people and parents will believe it is serious about overcoming the shortages and view the Government differently.

'Young people in our schools see the disadvantages and demands of teaching, and the stress their teachers are under. If they are to be attracted into the profession, such a package, implemented over an agreed period, would change the perception and reality of teaching.'

Britain has the worst schools in Europe

Education expert's damning conclusion

A devastating attack on the state of Britain's schools was launched by a distinguished international research body yesterday.

As pupils become the first in Europe to be sent home because of teacher shortages, the respected Organisation for Economic Co-operation and Development warned that the system could face 'meltdown'.

At the same time literacy levels among young people are among the worst in the industrialised world, with one in three lacking the basic skills to cope with everyday life, it said.

The spectre of a complete collapse of the traditional state school system was held up in the annual review of education policies among the OECD's 29 members around the world.

It blamed lack of recognition, red tape and poor working conditions for driving teachers out of the profession and warned that, as the exodus becomes worse, schools could find themselves trapped in a vicious circle of decline.

It also cast doubt on whether Government initiatives would solve the problem and held out the prospect of private companies stepping in to offer parents alternatives.

The report emerged as England's two main teaching unions continued a boycott of cover for vacant posts, which has already led to the cancellation of lessons for hundreds of pupils.

Heads' leaders have estimated that 10,000 teaching jobs are unfilled.

> *Literacy levels among young people are among the worst in the industrialised world, with one in three lacking the basic skills to cope with everyday life*

David Istance, the British expert who drew up the study, said he did not know of any other country in Europe where the crisis in teacher supply had resulted in children being sent home.

Mr Istance, principal administrator at the OECD's Centre for Educational Research and Innovation, said keeping teachers in the profession and making it a more attractive proposition were as important as training staff.

The introduction of performance pay to attract more talented graduates was unlikely to solve the problems, he warned.

'There are no magic keys to this. Salary by itself is not the first thing many teachers are concerned about, it is more to do with recognition and the conditions at work.

'In the UK it is about excessive amounts of paperwork and bureaucracy, which is something that makes it difficult to do what teachers want to do most.'

The study questioned whether the traditional school would continue to exist unless more could be done to attract people into teaching.

A separate OECD study showed the 'under-achievement' rates among 16- to 25-year-olds in Britain are worse than anywhere else in the EU, apart from Ireland.

It ranked 18 countries by the average scores in literacy tests of young school leavers between 1994 and 1998.

It also measured the literacy skills needed to cope with everyday

tasks at home or work, such as filling in forms or using bus and train timetables.

Britain scored poorly on both counts. It trailed in 14th place in levels of absolute literacy – well behind countries such as Germany, Holland and Canada – and ranked 13th on the second list.

The report said 35 per cent of young Britons completed their secondary education without achieving this basic standard.

This was nearly double the number in Germany and more than three times the level of functional illiteracy in Denmark and Finland.

Only Ireland, Poland, Hungary and the US had a poorer record.

The report is the first to study progress by the 29 OECD member countries towards improved 'lifelong learning' policies from nursery education to job training.

It ranked Britain only in the Third Division overall, saying it had 'comparatively weak and uneven performance' largely because of the scale of illiteracy among the adult workforce.

Sweden, Finland, Norway and Denmark were in the Premier league for education and training, followed by Canada, the Czech Republic, Germany, Holland and New Zealand.

The findings will be presented next week to a conference in Paris, which is due to be attended by Education Minister Baroness Blackstone.

The OECD was set up in 1960 to promote policies aimed at increasing economic growth and improve living standards in member countries.

Improving student performance

How English further education colleges can improve student retention and achievement

Over the last five years, further education colleges have helped a growing proportion of students to achieve their qualifications at the same time as supporting a big increase in student numbers. But further education colleges must make greater improvements in their student success rates, Sir John Bourn, Head of the National Audit Office, said today.

Overall success rates[1] – the proportion of qualification aims embarked upon that students successfully achieve – are only 56 per cent for 16-18s and 51 per cent for older

students. In his report to Parliament, Sir John identified a number of good practices which the best colleges use – such as helping students to choose the right course – which would help other colleges to improve their student retention and achievement rates.

The report found that the rate of student achievement has increased from 65 per cent in 1994-95 to 74 per cent in 1998-99 (the latest year for which data are available). This improvement is due in part to initiatives by the Department for Education and Employment (the Department) and the Further Education Funding Council (the Funding Council) aimed at improving teaching quality and providing incentives for colleges to raise retention and achievement rates. There are, however, significant variations in retention and – particularly – achievement rates between colleges. For general further education colleges and sixth form colleges, retention rates vary between 98 per cent and 72 per cent, and achievement rates vary between 98 per cent and 33 per cent. Although external factors such as the level of student deprivation and prior attainment of students explain part of the variation, other reasons include differences in ethos, systems, procedures and practices at individual colleges.

Some types of students find particular difficulty in achieving their qualifications. These include those employed for long hours of part-time work in parallel with their studies and students experiencing various kinds of deprivation.

The report makes a number of recommendations to colleges, and to the new Learning and Skills Council, on how to further improve student retention and achievement. These cover:

- helping students to choose the right course, for example by providing better pre-enrolment information about the financial and time demands of different courses;
- identifying and supporting students who are at greater risk of non-completion or non-achievement, for example by monitoring student absence closely and following up such absences promptly and sensitively;
- encouraging good quality teaching and learning methods, including providing prompt, regular and constructive feedback to students on their performance;
- helping students to develop good study techniques including providing advice on how to take notes effectively and how to set out written work coherently; and
- assessing performance by collecting better information on the reasons for non-completion and improving the timeliness of published data.

Sir John Bourn said today: 'Further education colleges, with the support of the Funding Council and the Department, have done well over the past five years to increase the proportion of students who achieve their qualifications. In particular

we were pleased to see that the number of colleges with overall achievement rates below 50 per cent has reduced dramatically.

'Overall success rates remain disappointing, however, and the gap between the best and worst performing colleges is still too wide. Poorer performing colleges need to adopt the good practices of the best if they are to help the Government meet the National Learning Targets.'

Notes

The further education sector provides a wide range of education and training opportunities to people from school leaving-age upwards. There are some 400 further education colleges in England, enabling 3.8 million students to study for some 17,000 different qualifications from about 480 awarding bodies, at a cost to the public purse of some £3 billion.

The Department for Education and Employment is responsible for

The betrayed generations

Standards in British schools 1950-2000. By Dr John Marks

In spite of the efforts of both political parties, the quality of state education in Britain remains worryingly low.

Standards fluctuate widely from school to school. At the age of seven, the average reading age of children in a school can vary by as much as 2 years; by the age of 14, this has increased to five years. As a result, many children are denied the opportunities which should be afforded to them. And this is in spite of the fact that, in real terms, more money is being spent on state education than ever before.

Dr John Marks, a lifelong campaigner for better standards in schools, presents an authoritative overview of standards in British education over the last 50 years. In *The Betrayed Generation: standards in British schools 1950 – 2000*, published by the Centre for Policy Studies, Dr Marks evaluates where we are now; asks how we got here; and suggests how things can be improved.

Dr Marks shows that 40% of the children who are entering secondary education are unable to read well enough to cope with the National Curriculum. By the age of 14, children are on average two years behind the standard expected of them. Despite the ever-rising trend in GCSE and A-level results, too many children are leaving school unable to read adequately or to do simple arithmetic.

Marks finds that the policy of comprehensivisation lies behind much of the decline in secondary school standards: he estimates that as many as 80,000 18-year-olds who would otherwise do well are failing to achieve 2 or more A-level passes.

The key to better state education is the rigorous setting and monitoring of standards. In addition, a more diverse and selective system of secondary education can also be expected to lead to an improvement in standards. Only then can we rectify a system in which too many children are condemned to a life of failure.

© Centre for Policy Studies

determining the overall policy for further education and the Further Education Funding Council is responsible for implementing it. From April 2001 a new Learning and Skills Council will replace the Further Education Funding Council and Training and Enterprise Councils. (Training and Enterprise Councils are private sector companies which manage local training and enterprise activities under a performance-based contract with the Secretary of State for Employment).

Source:

1 Success rates are the number of qualification aims achieved as a proportion of those started, even though students may subsequently have dropped them.

Achievement rates do not take account of qualifications started but not completed.

• The above information is a press release to launch the report *Improving Student Performance*, HC 276 2000-2001. 2 March 2001. ISBN: 0102839018. Price: £9.00. Report by the Comptroller and Auditor General.
© *UK National Audit Office*

Student drop outs cost £200m a year

By Lee Elliot Major

Student drop outs could be costing the taxpayer £200m a year, MPs were told yesterday. The estimate came from Professor Mantz Yorke, who produced the only major study on student drop outs two years ago, as he gave evidence to an inquiry into retention rates in universities by the House of Commons education committee. Official figures show that 17% of students fail to finish degrees, but drop-out rates vary dramatically for different universities and colleges.

Yorke, professor of education at Liverpool John Moores University, also called on universities to reform the first year of degree courses, which often involve examinations for students as early as the first term. Two-thirds of students bail out of degree courses during the first year. Yorke said that more support was needed for new students, particularly those from working-class backgrounds.

The committee's inquiry is to focus on why drop-out rates are so different for similar academic institutions.

Yorke said that £200m represented a ballpark figure for the annual cost of student drop outs in UK universities. But he added that the drop-out figures published by the higher education funding councils last year are likely to overestimate the extent of the problem. This is because the figures fail to take into account students who transfer after completing modules on degree courses.

The MPs also heard that the government's decision to scrap maintenance grants for student living costs is likely to have increased the drop-out rate in universities.

A particular concern is 'creeping debt' among students, said Yorke, with many students unaware of the mounting costs of university life until it is too late. But he added that students now spend more time in jobs to earn money while doing their degrees.

Yorke also warned that there was a conflict between the government's aims to attract more students from working-class backgrounds and to minimise student drop-out rates. 'We need to tackle access and non-completion together,' he said.

Two heads of higher education colleges, with two of the lowest drop-out rates in the sector, told the MPs that the removal of upfront fees would improve student retention.

Professor Michael Wright, principal of Canterbury Christ Church University College, said: 'Finding a way of removing the upfront costs of higher education and moving it towards a deferred contribution model is the thing I would most seriously consider.'

Dorma Urwin, principal of Worcester College of Higher Education, also said that students most likely to drop out of college were those enrolling with the least information on the course.

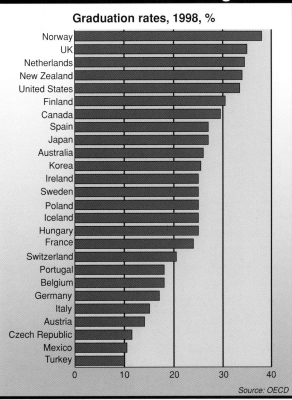

Universities and colleges

Graduation rates, 1998, %

Norway, UK, Netherlands, New Zealand, United States, Finland, Canada, Spain, Japan, Australia, Korea, Ireland, Sweden, Poland, Iceland, Hungary, France, Switzerland, Portugal, Belgium, Germany, Italy, Austria, Czech Republic, Mexico, Turkey

0   10   20   30   40

Source: OECD

Bread but no honey

Disappointing enrolments mean some of the new universities face cutbacks

By Donald MacLeod

A growing divide between the haves and have-nots in higher education emerges from the annual shareout of government funds for the coming year.

Announcing the distribution of £4.76bn for teaching and research, Sir Brian Fender, chief executive of the Higher Education Funding Council for England, said it was a 'good year' for universities and colleges.

The money available per student was going up 'for the first time in living memory'. 'British higher education is in a healthy state.'

But a number of new universities will suffer a cut in funding after failing to recruit enough students, and the settlement has done nothing to shake the vice-chancellors' conviction that the sector is £900m short of what it needs to do its job properly.

Meeting in Newcastle, Universities UK, which represents the heads of institutions, insisted on Friday that top-up fees were still an option – despite being ruled out by David Blunkett, the education secretary, and all the opposition political parties.

Paying the penalty for missing their recruitment targets are the universities of East London, Lincolnshire and Humberside, Luton, Nottingham Trent, South Bank, Sunderland and De Montfort.

The funding council has tried to cushion the blow by moderating the amount the worst-hit institutions lose under the formula for student numbers. Luton has been subsidised to the tune of more than £5m over the past two years. But universities are expected to take serious action to bring their finances back into balance. Luton is axing nearly 100 academic and administrative staff jobs. Lincolnshire and Humberside is to abandon its Hull campus and become the University of Lincoln. De Montfort is closing the Milton Keynes campus.

Among the biggest winners in this year's funding stakes are old-established Nottingham, which gets an extra £3.4m to teach additional students, Southampton (£2.5m), Leeds (£3.2m), Birmingham (£2.3m), Bristol, Durham, Essex, Exeter, Liverpool, Newcastle, Sheffield, Queen Mary and Westfield College London and Warwick which all receive more than £1m additional funding for increased numbers. These are the beneficiaries of the government's drive to expand numbers and the funding council's decision last year to relax the restrictions on how many students institutions were allowed to recruit.

> **'We have an increasingly well-informed student population who are careful about where they go'**

There were many more 18-year-olds on the market to take up places.

It is not all gloom for new universities, however. Teesside is awarded a rise of more than £2m for additional students, while Leeds Metropolitan and Plymouth also gain substantially.

Sir Brian said some universities and colleges were having to work hard to fill their places, but overall demand was rising. It was inevitable that some universities would be doing better than others in recruitment: 'We have an increasingly well-informed student population who are careful about where they go.'

The picture is complicated by the continued unpopularity of science and engineering among school and college leavers, which appears to have hit both old and new universities. Prestigious Imperial College London suffered a £1.8m holdback this year because it failed to meet its recruitment targets. Professor Rees Rawlings, pro-rector, blamed the shortfall on the 5% decline in students taking maths and physics at A-level.

Some of the biggest gainers are not conventional universities. A massive 9% increase (nearly £8m) goes to the Open University, and further education colleges get a 6.5%

rise in funding for higher education, against an average 4% rise for all institutions.

The lion's share of the new foundation degrees announced by Blunkett are due to be delivered in further education colleges (collaborating with universities). These grants also reflect the government's goal of promoting part-time degrees as a way of increasing participation to its goal of 50% of young people under 30.

Part-time courses are not proving as attractive as predicted. More than 14,000 new part-time places funded by the council in England last year remained unfilled (most on sub-degree courses like Higher National Diplomas). Sir Brian predicts that the government's

targets will be met by a greater proportion of full-time students than in the original targets.

Scotland has already passed the Blair target: by 1999/2000 58% of 17-30-year-olds were in higher education or had participated.

Over the next 10 years the number of 18- to 20-year-olds in England is set to rise by 10%, compelling the funding council to find more places even if the government were not committed to increasing the proportion of young people in higher education. On past trends, school and college leavers are looking for full-time courses – which will reinforce the advantage of the old universities. Numbers in the older age group (25-29) who have

been more interested in part-time courses will drop rapidly.

• For students applying to start degree courses in September this year, the funding announcement is good news. Universities and colleges in England are being funded to take an extra 20,400 full-time and 32,300 part-time places, though there were more than 5,000 full-time places left unfilled last September. Of course there are more 18- to 20-year-olds around in the population but on balance institutions are looking for candidates and will be more likely to negotiate if your grades do not quite match your offers. There should also be places available through clearing.

© Guardian Newspapers Limited 2001

Fair deal?

In 2001-2 Edinburgh will spend nearly £1,400 more on each student than Westminster – and £1,600 more than Cardiff. Stephen Court reports on the disturbing fallout of devolution

Consider yourself lucky if you were born in Scotland and plan to study at a Scottish university. The Scottish Executive will spend about a quarter more on your education than will be spent on students in England and Wales. You won't have to pay up-front tuition fees. Some of you will be eligible for a non-repayable grant to help with living costs. And, for students on standard full-time first degree courses, you will have four years at university, compared with three years in other parts of the UK.

Other attractions could include having the television chef Clarissa Dickson Wright as the rector of your university, if you go to Aberdeen, or sharing a lecture theatre at St Andrews with Prince William.

The sharpest funding differences in the UK are shown in the unit of funding resource for each full-time equivalent student. Next year, the unit of resource for all expenditure (recurrent and non-recurrent) in cash terms will be £5,360 for each student in England, £5,138 in Wales, and £6,744 in Scotland. Information for Northern Ireland was not available at the time of writing.

The unit will rise by slightly over 5% in England and Scotland, but only 3.5% in Wales. Once you have taken inflation at 2.5% into account for next year, the Welsh increase is only a little bit above the rate of inflation.

Spending next year in Scotland will be around 2% above inflation, spending in England will be 0.4% above inflation, and spending in Wales will be around 0.4% below inflation

---

In terms of the unit of recurrent funding alone, which gives a clearer picture of what is actually being spent on the education of each student, spending next year in Scotland will be around 2% above inflation, spending in England will be 0.4% above inflation, and spending in Wales will be around 0.4% below inflation – a real-terms cut, in other words.

This in itself is a remarkable improvement on the past decade and more, which has seen consistent real-terms cuts in spending for each student in the UK. But why is spending per student more than a quarter higher in Scotland than in England or Wales? Why are the recurrent increases higher for Scotland than for England and Wales?

It is not that Scotland has a proportionately lower number of students. In fact, 46% of young people in Scotland participated in higher education in 1997-98, compared with 32% in England and Wales, and 44% in Northern Ireland.

The answer lies in post-devolution funding decisions, and in the historical differences in spending baselines in each country, which may have been accentuated by the application of the so-called Barnett formula. This formula was introduced in 1978 as a means of linking levels of change in funding in England to funding in Scotland, Wales and Northern Ireland. It is based on population levels. The accuracy of the formula, and the extent to which its application may have benefited non-English parts of the UK – particularly Scotland – is a matter of controversy. But whatever the reason, spending per student in Scotland is way ahead of England and Wales.

What must be galling to students in England and Wales is the fact that, while the amount spent on them lags behind Scottish students, they – like students in Northern Ireland – are having to pay up-front tuition fees for full-time undergraduate courses.

Recent student support measures from David Blunkett's Department for Education and Employment mean that in 2001-2 only half the undergraduates in England and Wales will be liable to pay fees. But that's still 50% more than in Scotland, where fees were abolished from autumn 2000.

The fissures in the UK caused by Scottish students in England, Wales or Northern Ireland having to pay fees, and English, Welsh and Northern Ireland students in Scotland also having to pay fees – unlike EU students – underline the impact of devolution.

Students north of Hadrian's Wall aren't getting away scot-free: they will have to pay a graduate endowment of £2,000 once they are income-earners. But this is about a third less than tuition fees elsewhere in the UK over the three years of a typical first degree. Since it is contingent on income, the Scottish endowment will be easier to pay than the up-front lump-sum tuition fee. And the burden on Scottish families while they are supporting students through higher education will be smaller.

And what is more, from 2001-2 non-repayable cost of living bursaries, to a maximum of £2,000 a year, will be available to young students from poor families in Scotland. And about 30,000 mature students entering higher education for the first time will benefit from discretionary bursaries.

It's a matter of attitude, as much as anything. The Scottish Executive, in last year's report *Scotland: The Learning Nation*, said: 'The fear of debt is a possible disincentive to students from lower income families entering higher education. A key objective of our new scheme is therefore to reduce the amount of loan students need to take out over the period of their study.'

Because of this, the executive is prepared to find resources from elsewhere to compensate institutions for the loss of tuition fees and fund a limited reintroduction of maintenance grants.

'How can we ensure that no student is deterred from taking up or completing his/her studies due to financial hardship?'

Some vice-chancellors in England have questioned whether the position in Scotland is sustainable. The Scottish Executive estimates that the cost of these changes for HE and FE will be about £50m a year, 2% of the total budget for the Department of Enterprise and Lifelong Learning in 2001-2.

It should be manageable – particularly since the additional cash funding for higher education in Scotland from grant and fees in 2001-2 will be £53m (and £24m in 2002-3 and £27m in 2003-4). In the long run, the cost of the abolition of fees will be offset by the full projected income of £16m a year from the graduate endowment scheme. Since the Scottish participation rate is near the government's 50% target, less extra funding will be needed than in England and Wales.

With devolution, it is likely that levels of public spending will increasingly diverge. A Treasury report notes: 'Responsibility for United Kingdom fiscal policy, macroeconomic policy and public expenditure allocation across the United Kingdom will remain with the Treasury. As a result, the devolved administrations' budgets will continue to be determined within the framework of public expenditure control in the United Kingdom. However once overall public expenditure budgets have been determined, the devolved administrations will have freedom to make their own spending decisions on devolved programmes within the overall totals.'

While education and employment secretary David Blunkett adopts a policy in England of ameliorating the impact of the introduction of tuition fees and the end of the maintenance grant, views in other parts of the UK are changing. The Welsh Assembly's education and lifelong learning committee is conducting a review of higher education in Wales. The review asks: 'How can we ensure that no student is deterred from taking up or completing his/her studies due to financial hardship?' This includes assessing whether students should contribute financially towards tuition. The results of the review will be available in the spring.

Meanwhile the minister for education and lifelong learning in Wales, Jane Davidson, is setting up an independent inquiry into student hardship and funding in Wales, to tackle problems in the current system of student maintenance and support.

The Northern Ireland Assembly's committee for higher and further education, training and employment has proposed a system similar to Scotland's, with the abolition of up-front tuition fees, graduate contributions to tuition, and means-tested non-repayable cost of living bursaries. Although higher education minister Sean Farren has not gone along with abolishing tuition fees, it may be that the example of Scotland and developments in Wales will create sufficient pressure to make him change his mind. That could just leave England as a bastion of the Blunkett-inspired system of tuition fees and no maintenance grant. But with a general election in the offing, who knows what will happen?

• Stephen Court is senior research officer at the Association of University Teachers

Building for the future

After years of neglect, money is being spent on school buildings, their infrastructure and, in some cases, new schools, as the government gets the education system fit for the 21st century

The last three years has seen a complete sea change in the amount of money being ploughed into improving school buildings and schools. David Blunkett recently announced that investment in school buildings this year would be £2 billion, nearly three times the amount spent in 1996-7.

This capital spending on schools will rise to £2.5 billion in 2001-2 and £3.2 billion the year after, giving a total of just under £8 billion for the three years until 2003-4. This is the biggest investment in schools for decades.

The spending programme is the amount needed to redress the backlog of repairs, maintenance and modernisation of 7,000 schools in England and the rebuilding of 650 schools.

The total also includes a larger allowance for capital devolved directly to schools, started in April: up to £16,000 a year for the typical primary school and £50,000 a year for the typical secondary school by 2003-4. This money is to help maintain schools and will have increased from £6,500 and £19,000 respectively.

It also includes £1.65 billion on Private Finance Initiatives, which has enabled new schools such as Milton Cross in Portsmouth to be built and the renovation of many others.

'Many of our schools have risen to the challenge of raising standards, but good schools also need good buildings. We have acted to tackle a backlog of repairs and have already seen vital work to 11,000 schools and have started work on 6,000 more,' David Blunkett says.

'We will provide up to 7,000 schools with new roofs and classrooms, removing temporary classrooms and modernising buildings. We will also see work start on 650 new, overhauled or replacement schools across England.

'Since 1997, this government has acted to address the pressing needs of thousands of schools across England. Much remains to be done, but we can see the results of a reversal in the decline of school buildings, with major new investment in classrooms and schools.

'The work we have begun will ensure that future generations of children can be taught in good schools with high standards of learning as well as a safe, maintained environment.'

Wired for action in the classroom

The government is investing £1 billion to ensure schools have access to the latest computer technology.

The money will ensure there is a computer for every eight pupils in primary schools and for every five pupils in secondary schools by the end of the period.

In September, the Prime Minister announced £750 million of new funding to help realise this aim. This builds on £245 million from the final phase of a National Grid for Learning programme, and £155 million from the Standards Fund. The £1 billion is being invested in schools in the three years until 2004.

Already, previous investment has helped raise school internet connections from 6,500 in 1998 to over 20,000 now, or 88 per cent of all schools.

• The above information is an extract from *Teachers Magazine* which is produced by the Department for Education and Employment and can be accesed on the internet at www.dfee.gov.uk/teacher/

The student of 2000: more work, less play

Universities are very different from a generation ago – studying is only half the battle for many would-be graduates, says Roderick Floud

Who is the modern student? The athlete with his college scarf? The blue-stocking, cycling to her lecture? The activist hurling abuse at a politician?

These days, the students you are most likely to meet are the checkout girl at Sainsbury's or the waiter in your favourite bistro.

The modern student works: 'full-time student' no longer means someone who spends time in libraries or lectures, with an occasional vacation job. At many universities, most students have jobs during term-time. At London Guildhall, more than 80 per cent of our students work during term for between five and 25 hours a week.

Why do they do it? For some, it is certainly to fund a car or to finance evenings in the pub. For many, however, whose families are too poor to help, it is to keep body and soul together. Some have a natural aversion to building up a large debt to the Student Loans Company. Many mature students feel guilty about their wives, husbands or children supporting them during a college course, and work to reduce the burden.

Juggling study with work is hard. It requires skills of time management that would be envied by many management consultants. As one student, Aidan, put it to me: 'I need lectures to start at 10am, not because of a party the night before but because then I can use a cheap railcard. I must be away by 4pm to pick up my daughter, leave her with her gran, and get to my evening job. When do I write my essays? Well, there's the weekend and early mornings.'

Many students still live in college rooms or halls of residence. But others stay at or close to home, where jobs are easier to come by. Often, they commute to classes and live in cramped accommodation, a shared room where there is nowhere to study. There is not enough money for books, let alone a computer. It is no surprise that they sometimes wonder if they can cope or will be forced to drop out.

If this is the modern student, what does it mean for the modern university? At London Guildhall, 48 per cent of our students are over 21 when they start to study with us; more than 90 per cent come from state schools or colleges, and 35 per cent come from families of manual workers. Most are the first generation of their families to go to university and many have parents whose native language is not English.

Our job is to help these students to learn, to make sure their degree is worth as much as a degree from any other university and to help them get a job at the end.

Mostly we succeed, though it often takes longer than the ideal three years; students repeat years or semesters, put off examinations while they care for a sick child or parent, change course to one that suits them better. Sometimes they, and we, fail; it is rarely because the student is not intelligent enough, but because the pressures on them are too great.

Some students are academic high-flyers who just need to be shown the way to the library or the laboratory. But many at London Guildhall find study a challenge; they may even have failed before.

For some, the problem is dyslexia; we provide training in using voice-input computers, to overcome spelling difficulties. For others, it is time management or note-taking; for yet others their maths is not good enough for a course in economics or accounting. Teaching of the basic subject is just part of the overall package that we must provide.

Even before the students arrive, we run financial helplines. More than half are from lower-income families and pay no fees, but they need guidance through the maze of loan and grant schemes. They need advice on their careers; mature and ethnic minority students still find it particularly difficult to get jobs. It is not a matter of advising them on which accountancy firm to join, but of painstakingly working with small businesses who have never employed a graduate before.

At times it doesn't work. Statistics show that, in some universities, more than a quarter of

> *Juggling study with work is hard. It requires skills of time management that would be envied by many management consultants*

students fail to complete their courses, although many return to study later on. It is easy to say: 'You shouldn't have admitted them in the first place!'

With perfect hindsight, perhaps this is true, but would you want your son or daughter, perhaps struggling to get A-levels, told that

they could not even try a college course; would you want to say it to someone who sees university as the only chance of escape from a dead-end job?

All British universities exist to give people a chance. One must not compromise standards, for that would short-change our students. So we have to help them in ways which, when I went to university 40 years ago, were unheard of. We struggle, sometimes we even despair, but I know that, each year, I will get from a student such as Aidan a letter with the magic words: 'You have changed my life.'

• Roderick Floud is provost of London Guildhall University

Student earners lose out twice

By Lee Elliot Major

A quarter of students doing part-time work while at university are earning below the national minimum wage and their academic work is suffering, MPs were told yesterday.

According to a report presented by Professor Claire Callender from South Bank University, three in five students now take paid work during academic courses, working an average of 11 hours a week. But 40% of those using part-time jobs to finance their studies reported that their academic performance had suffered as a consequence, and 25% were paid below the national minimum wage.

The comments came during the latest hearing of the House of Commons education committee's inquiry into the factors affecting student drop-out rates.

The committee heard that as many as two-fifths of mature students without A-levels drop out of university courses in engineering, maths, computing and the physical sciences.

A submission to the inquiry from the Higher Education Funding Council for England argues that the main factors influencing student drop-out rates before 1997 were A-level grades, age of students and degree subjects. Mature students with no A-levels for example are twice as likely to drop out than average in science and engineering subjects.

The committee heard concerns that the government's interpretation of loans as extra income for students was completely out of touch with the views of students themselves who see loans as extra debts.

There have been suggestions that the Department for Education and Employment tried to hush up

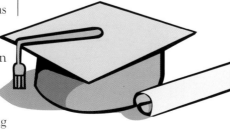

some of the more damaging conclusions of Professor Callender's report originally published last month. The DfEE-commissioned study found that student debts had trebled, and nearly nine out of ten students now face financial difficulties. Yet the DfEE summary of the report focused on the extra income available to students.

'Whether it [the DfEE statement] reports the overall findings of the report is open to question,' Professor Callender told the MPs. 'My concern is that there is enough evidence that suggests that they [students] view loans as debts.'

Professor Callender said she was 'deeply concerned' that the move from grants to loans in the student funding system would deter students from going to university. She complained that there was no research available that looked at the impact of student finances on university access and drop-out rates over time. She added that her study suggested strong links between academic achievement, debt and financial hardship.

Frequently asked questions

Information from the Department for Education and Employment (DfEE)

How do I apply for financial help?

There are four basic steps in the process of applying for student support:

Step one – Get an application form (also known as an HE1 form). You can obtain a form from:

a) your Local Education Authority (LEA) – ask them to send you a form or

b) your school or college may have copies of the form,

c) the DfEE web site – use the electronic application form which can be accessed from the DfEE *Planning to go into higher education?* page of their web site which can be found at www.dfee.gov.uk/studentsupport/ student_planning_he.cfm

Step two – Complete your application form – and return it to your LEA. Your LEA will let you know whether you are eligible for help with your tuition fees and a student loan. If you are, they will send you a Financial Form (also known as an HE2 form).

Step three – Complete the financial form – and return it to your LEA promptly. Based on the information you include on this form, your LEA will tell you how much, if anything, you and your family will have to contribute towards your fees and your living costs and the maximum amount of student loan you can borrow.

Step four – Apply for your loan – you must complete and send the Loan Request Form, supplied by your LEA, to the Student Loan Company telling them how much you want to borrow.

These steps are explained in detail in the publication *Financial Support for Higher Education Students in 2001/2002*. You can get a copy of this booklet from your LEA, or from the DfEE information line on 0800 731 9133.

When can I apply for help?

You can apply as soon as possible after applying for your course and up to four months after your course starts. The earlier you apply the more likely it will be that your money will be available for you to collect at the start of your course.

How much loan can I get?

The maximum amount of loan that you can get in 2001/2002 is:

- £3,815 for students living away from home
- £4,700 for students in London and living away from home
- £3,020 for students living at home

75% of the maximum loan is available to all eligible students regardless of any other income they have. Whether you can get any or all of the remaining 25% depends on your income and that of your family. This will be assessed by your LEA.

How is my loan paid?

The Student Loans Company (SLC) will usually pay your loan in three instalments. Payments are made either by cheque or directly into your bank or building society account. You will receive a payment schedule from the SLC which tells you how you will get your money.

How does the repayment process work?

You will be liable to begin making repayments on your loan from the April after you leave your course. If you pay tax through PAYE your employer will be required to make deductions from your salary once you earn over the repayment threshold of £10,000 a year. If you are self-employed you will be required to make your repayments with your tax return. Your repayments will be calculated at 9% of your income over the £10,000 threshold. For example, someone with an income of £11,000 a year would be liable to repay 9% of £1,000 or £90 a year. Someone else earning £20,000 a year would be liable to repay £900 a year. It is also possible to make extra voluntary repayments in order to speed up the repayment process.

Details of how the loan repayment process works can be found in the DfEE booklet *Student Loans; Guidance on Terms and Conditions*. You can get a copy of this booklet from the DfEE information line on 0800 731 9133.

What if I don't get a job after leaving my course or if I lose my job?

You will only be required to make repayments on your student loan if you are earning more than £10,000 a year. If your income falls below this level your repayments will cease and will not start again until your income is above £10,000 a year.

How much will I have to pay towards my fees?

That depends on your, and your family's, income. The most you will have to pay is £1,075. If your parents' residual income is less than £20,000 you will pay nothing. If their income is above £29,784 you will have to pay the full £1,075. We estimate that around 50% of students will not have to pay fees in 2001/2002. Your LEA will assess how much, if anything, you will have to pay.

How will I pay my fees?

Your college will ask you for any fee contribution assessed by your LEA. You will pay your college directly. Many colleges allow students to pay their fees by instalments. Please check with individual colleges to find out what their fee payment policy is.

What extra help is available?

Extra help may be available from your LEA if you are disabled, have dependants, have been in care or if you have extra travel costs to meet.

Details of the extra help available in 2001/2002 can be found in section 2 of *Financial Support for Higher Education Students in 2001/2002*, copies of which can be obtained from the DfEE information line on 0800 731 9133.

Extra help, in the form of an Access or Opportunity bursary, a hardship loan or help from hardship funds may also be available from your college or university. Contact the admissions tutors or student support service at your university or college for further details. Further details can also be found in section 4 of *Financial Support for Higher Education Students in 2001/2002*.

I want to study part time. What help is available for me?

Part-time students on low incomes, or on benefits, can apply to have their fees paid for them. A £500 loan to help with course costs is also available. Further details on help available for part-time students can be accessed at the *Part Time Student* page of the DfEE website.

Part-time students with disabilities may be able to get help from Disabled Student Allowances (DSAs). Further details of who is eligible for DSAs can be accessed from the *Students with disabilities* page on the DfEE web site at www.dfee.gov.uk/studentsupport/student_disabled.cfm

What if I change course or university/college?

You should tell your LEA of any changes as soon as possible. A change of course or university/college might affect whether you are able to get financial help and how much you can get. A change of details form is accessible from the DfEE website at www.dfee.gov.uk/student_loans/default.htm   *© Crown Copyright*

Students being excluded

Increasing numbers of students excluded over fees non-payment

Thousands of students are being excluded from universities because they are unable to pay tuition fees, a university vice-chancellor said yesterday.

Peter Knight, vice-chancellor of the University of Central England in Birmingham, told a conference of university heads that they faced a serious problem of student debt, with increasing numbers of students dropping out of courses at universities.

'I estimate that several thousand students are not completing courses because they can't pay fees,' he said. Dr Knight added that the loss of maintenance grants for living costs was the biggest factor leading to increasing student drop-out rates. Many students were using loans to pay fees when they were intended for food and rent.

The clearest sign yet of the deepening levels of debt faced by students was a 15% drop in the

By Lee Elliot Major

revenue from university student bars at UCE over the last year, Dr Knight said. He said that a total of 197 students had been excluded from UCE last year.

The comments came at the annual meeting of the higher education funding council for England, the government body which allocates teaching and research grants to universities.

Dr Knight is the second university head in a week to warn that student debt has risen sharply since the government introduced fees and scrapped maintenance grants three years ago.

Diana Green, vice-chancellor of Sheffield Hallam University, told MPs on the House of Commons education committee that the

number of students dropping out of university because of debt is increasing every year.

A report for university heads last July estimated that £21m in fee payments from students was outstanding. Students graduating last year were the first to be charged the £1,050 annual fee for their degree courses.

Dr Knight said that universities were witnessing a new underclass of students 'who didn't know where the next meal was coming from'. He said that some students now face 'grinding poverty'.

Students from households with an annual income of between £15,000 and £30,000 were struggling the most, according to Dr Knight. These students have to pay contributions to fees, but also find it hard to get any extra money from parents to help them through their university careers.

© Guardian Newspapers Limited 2001

Students living in Scotland

Frequently asked questions

Can I get help from Students Awards Agency Scotland (SAAS) for my course?
If you are a Scottish domiciled student or an EU student studying on a course that we support, you may be eligible for student support.

Which courses qualify?
Most full-time HNC, HND or first degree courses qualify, as well as Postgraduate Certificates of Education; some postgraduate courses; and the Scottish Studentship Scheme.

What if my course is not one of these?
You may be able to get help from your college or from the education department of your local council.

Where do I get more information and an application form?
You can get forms and SAAS information booklets from colleges and universities, careers offices, schools and the education department of your local council.

What help can I get?
We can help with tuition fees and support for living costs.

What help do I get for fees?
If you are eligible, we will pay your tuition fees directly to your college/university. But you must apply so that we can assess you and confirm whether you are eligible.

If you are studying at an institution outside Scotland we will 'means-test' your tuition fees and the amount we pay will depend on your own/your parents'/or your spouse's income. The amount we pay could be less than the cost of the tuition fees and you will have to pay the difference.

The tuition fees we pay represent only about a quarter of the actual cost of a course. The Government pays the remaining cost directly to the college or university.

We pay a maximum amount towards postgraduate students' tuition fees (currently £2,740). If your fees are higher than that, you will have to pay the difference.

What is living cost support?
Living cost support is for the cost of your food and accommodation, books, clothes, some travelling costs etc.

If you started your course in session 1997/98, and have been on a continuous programme of study since then, you will most likely receive help with living costs through grants and loans.

If you started your course in session 1998/99, 1999/2000 or 2000/2001 support for living costs is through a partly means-tested student loan plus any non-repayable supplementary grants, depending on your circumstances.

I have already been on a course. Will I still be eligible for assistance?
Previous assistance can affect your eligibility for help towards fees.

If you already hold a degree-level qualification, you may not get any help towards your fees.

If you have completed an HNC, you may get assistance to do an HND or degree-level course.

If you have completed an HND, you may get support from the second year of a degree-level course.

You can still apply for a student loan for your living costs.

Contact the Agency for advice about your particular circumstances.

When should I apply?
Before starting your course, apply as soon as you have received your unconditional offer of a place from

FEES
BOOKS
FOOD
RENT

the college or university, or a conditional offer for your first choice of course.

If you are already on a course, apply as early as possible. If you want to be sure that your loan or grant will be paid at the start of the next session, send your form to us by 15 May.

When will I know what I will get?
We acknowledge receipt of all applications, and we aim to process them within 28 days. Then, when we have assessed your application, we will send you a Letter of Award explaining what support you will get. If you have applied for a loan, the Student Loans Company Ltd will send you a payment schedule setting out the arrangements for your loan.

When will I get the payment?
Payment for loan and grant is made in 3 instalments, at the start of each term.

We aim to have your first instalment of loan or grant available for you to collect at your institution on the first day of term, provided you sent your application in good time. It is very important to complete the application form correctly, ensuring that it is signed where necessary, and enclosing any relevant documentation. We return incomplete forms for completion, which can cause delay.

What do I do if I need to speak to someone about my loan?
Get in touch with the Student Loans Company Ltd, at 100 Bothwell Street Glasgow, G2 7JD, Freephone 0800 405010

What if my parents don't want to give you information about their income?
They don't have to, but if you are studying in Scotland you can still apply for your tuition fees. If you are studying outside Scotland you will have to pay all of your tuition fees.

In either case, you will only be able to apply for the non means-tested part of the loan.

I have been in care up till now. Can I get extra help?
You may be entitled to extra help for the summer holidays. Contact us for more information.

I have a disability. Can I get any extra help?
Yes. The Disabled Students' Allowance is available for things like special equipment. This allowance is not means-tested. Contact us for more information.

Can I get any help for travelling to and from my college or university?
SAAS can contribute towards the cost of daily travel to your college or university. If you study away from home, we may also pay the cost of travel between your home and term-time address at the start and end of each term (i.e. a maximum of three return journeys a year).

What travel expenses will SAAS pay?
Travel expenses are subject to certain limits. The maximum costs, which we will consider when assessing payment of travel claims, are: for single students living at home £3.00 per day plus £495. For married students living in their own home it is £3.00 per day plus £695.

For single students living away from home it is £3.00 per day plus the cost of six single journeys to and from your term-time address.

We deduct a 'travel element' from all claims. This represents the cost of travel which students are expected to meet themselves from either their loan, maintenance grant or their own resources. For those still being assisted under the previous scheme, the deduction is £80. For everyone else it is £155.

If you are subject to a student, parental or spouse contribution which is greater than the amount of means-tested loan and supplementary grants you are eligible for, the difference will be deducted from your travel entitlement.

If your approved expenses come to less than the maximum given above, you will be paid the lesser amount.

We will only pay for the most economical fares available for the type of transport used. Where the cheapest fares are available under the Student Railcard or Bus Pass schemes, we will pay you for the cheapest rate plus the cost of the railcard/bus pass.

Who can claim?
In general, most students (apart from EU students) can claim for travelling expenses.

But, the grant is means-tested and we can only assess it if you have provided your/your parents' or spouse's income details. If you have only claimed for fees or the non means-tested student loan, and want to apply for travelling expenses, ask the Agency for a form for you to provide the income details we need.

If you live within reasonable walking distance of the university/college you should not claim this grant.

Where can I get an application form?
We send claim forms (AB4) to colleges/universities in December each year. Send your completed form to the Agency as soon as possible after the end of your first term.

When do I get my expenses?
If we receive your claim form by 31 January 2001, and you have completed it correctly, we will send payment to your college or university for collection at the start of the third term. If you send it after this date your payment may be delayed.

If you are experiencing financial hardship, we may pay you up to 50% advance of your estimated expenses. Write to the Agency explaining your circumstances, as we assess each case on its own merits.

• The above information is from the The Student Awards Agency for Scotland, 3 Redheughs Rigg, South Gyle, Edinburgh, EH12 9YT. Web site www.student-support-saas.gov.uk/

Students learn a hard lesson about debt

The Government has set up a debt task force, but at the same time it is piling the pressure on students, says Jenny Knight

The National Association of Citizens' Advice Bureaux is concerned about the increasing number of consumers becoming bogged down by unmanageable debt. The Government has responded by calling on lenders to sort out the mess and has set up a debt task force.

Yet, while the Department of Trade and Industry investigates the problems of people who cannot manage their debts, the Government is actively encouraging another group to borrow more. Following the abolition of grants in favour of loans, plus the imposition of tuition fees on all but the poorest, the student debt burden grows every year. And students have the least immediate chance of repaying the money.

As a nation we owe £70 billion on our credit cards and in personal loans, and a further £600 billion in mortgage borrowings. But competition is gradually eroding interest rates charged on credit cards and personal loans, and the amount owed on overdrafts actually fell by £105 million in the latest quarter.

Student borrowing, on the other hand, rose by 17.5 per cent last year, with 73.3 per cent of undergraduates and 76 per cent of postgraduates struggling with debt. The National Union of Students says the average student owes £5,286 at the end of their course.

A survey by Barclays showed that six out of 10 graduates owed money to the Student Loan Company, and six out of 10 also owed money to their bank. It is hardly surprising, then, that the student drop-out rate grew over the same period from 14 to 18 per cent.

Student debt has been rising over the past 10 years, since loans were introduced. In September, annual tuition fees rose to £1,050. Very little is yet known about the long-term effects of this early descent into debt or how long it takes the average graduate to move into credit.

Some fear that running up debt with no early prospect of repayment actually encourages a devil-may-care attitude to money. Dr Ron Roberts, health psychologist at the University of Westminster, says that debt makes students anxious and depressed with low vitality and lack of enthusiasm for social activities.

Student debt has been rising over the past 10 years, since loans were introduced

---

He found that students spend ever more time working for extra cash. About seven in 10 work through the summer vacation and half continue to do so during term time. He concludes that working harms a student's academic progress, which leads to stress.

Dr Roberts' research suggested that debt even drove some students to crime. With a colleague, Dr John Golding, he found that some third-year students had debts of up to £9,000. They fear that, with the new tuition fees, debt among third years could this year rise to £12,000, or even £15,000.

Dr Roberts said: 'The notion that students are having a fantastic time is wrong. They are being driven into enforced indebtedness and no one has looked at the long-term consequences.

'If I had just taken my A levels, I don't think university would be an automatic choice. More and more employees are becoming sceptical about the worth of degrees and today's graduates have a poorer chance of well-paid jobs than they did some years back.'

Professor Paul Webley, an economic psychologist at Exeter University, agrees that a degree no longer guarantees a well-paid job. He said: 'Some students believe they are going to be high earners. But many overestimate their post-graduate earnings.

'If they see something in the paper about huge salaries for new graduates in banking, they think they will be earning that salary. They don't look at statistics for average graduate salaries or for the numbers who are unemployed. Most people are over-optimistic about their prospects, including their financial ones.'

Prof Webley found that most graduates failed to achieve the level of income they had been expecting. He said: 'The idea that being a graduate will boost earnings is becoming a myth. Now that one in three school leavers goes to university, it is just not true that every graduate will benefit financially.'

Prof Webley advises students to view a student loan as something akin to a mortgage. People don't think of mortgages as debt, he said, but rather as planned expenditure which will be paid off in a number of years.

Viewed in that way, the loan would not encourage students to see debt as a normal way of life, he said.

Those that do so are in danger of borrowing even more money. He said: 'Some people think that, because they're in debt with no hope of repaying it, they might as well borrow more.'

It is not clear whether this psychological problem causes debt or is a consequence of debt, but there is evidence that being in debt may change people's attitudes and opinions, he said. However, a study of a group of people in debt revealed that roughly one-third went on to become chronic debtors, one-third returned to credit over time and the remainder fell somewhere between the two extremes.

Student loans do not have to be repaid until the graduate's earnings reach a certain level. However, the generous overdraft terms offered to students by banks do not continue into perpetuity. Banks are keen to attract both undergraduate and graduate accounts, and offer a variety of low-interest and interest-free deals.

Often parents are more worried than their offspring about the high level of debt they are forced into. Sophie Brookes, development director of National Debt Line, said: 'An increasing number of calls come from parents with children in their teens and early 20s.'

The British Bankers' Association insists that the majority of the population has no problem dealing with debt. Others begin to have problems only when their circumstances change – if they lose a job, are divorced or bereaved, for instance – while others become over-committed after taking poor advice. And then, at the extreme end of the spectrum, come the credit-junkies and the fraudsters.

But the National Association of Citizens' Advice Bureaux says the number of people seeking help with debt problems rose by 16 per cent this year. Bureaux in England and Wales handled nearly one million debt enquiries. A spokesman for the association said: 'This brings the increase over the past two years to an alarming 37 per cent, fuelling fears that people are being encouraged to borrow more than they can afford.'

The DTI task force will look at how to:

- Make lenders explain credit terms more clearly
- Draw up a lenders' code of practice, which would include looking at an applicant's total borrowing commitments and his or her ability to repay them
- Prevent lenders from offering interest-free or low-interest loans which depend on a host of confusing and onerous require-ments that leave borrowers having to pay much higher rates because they have failed to comply with the terms of the offer.

© *Telegraph Group Limited, London 2000*

Work

Information from studentUK

Let's face it . . . it takes a lot of effort to find a part-time job, but once you do, it'll be worthwhile.

Ideally you'll find a job that is in some way related to your course or your career, that will look stunning on your CV. Even if the job isn't that exciting and involves cleaning or working in a shop, you'll still be able to get valuable teamwork experience and time-management skills.

Here are a few hints that have been recommended to studentUK:

Temping agencies
Hotrecruit (www.hotrecruit.co.uk)
Specialise in temporary work and even have a 'crazy' section where the jobs range from croupier to game show host.

Tempz (www.tempz.com)
Gives you your own web page within their site to show yourself off to employers. Has a rate match to show how much you are worth.

4Moonlighters
(www.4moonlighters.com)
Introduces those with spare work capacity to those in need of additional or part-time specialist skills.

Student brand managers
a) FMCG Field Marketing also employ students at every university in the UK and the work is all local and flexible. You'll get to work at some cool exhibitions and festivals and do cigarette and alcohol promotions. Ring (01844) 337400 for more details.
b) Get Real! are a marketing agency that employs students to represent companies such as IPC magazines, NME, Red Bull and Internet search engines like Lycos to name but a few. Call them for more details on 07000 438732.
c) The *Guardian* runs a student brand manager scheme, but you have to get in quick because they get a lot of applications.

Action watching jobs
Your local theatre or cinema and even football stadium have lots of interesting jobs available and you get to watch the action at the same time. Contact them directly and see.

Student Union
Student Union jobs are hard to come by and usually low paid but at least you don't have far to go and can see your friends at the same time. See someone at your Student Union as soon as you start the year, for the best choice of positions. If you are interested in the media, look at working on your student newspaper or radio station. You might even like to help out with the entertainment and get in for free.

Shop work
Working in clothes shops or supermarkets may get you a staff discount so at least you can save on essentials.

© *studentUK 2001*

Student living report

The first definitive study of the 'Student Experience'

The inaugural *Student Living Report*, published today, represents one of the most comprehensive quantitative surveys of full-time undergraduate and postgraduate students. The findings are derived from the first in-depth, definitive study of 'student experience' including issues relating to academic studies, personal finances, accommodation, social life and post-study aspirations.

The survey was commissioned by the UNITE Group plc, UK's leading specialist provider of student accommodation services and an independent provider of key worker accommodation for NHS Trusts.

MORI (Market & Opinion Research International) conducted the survey on behalf of UNITE, among 1,103 full-time undergraduate and postgraduate students at 22 universities across England, Scotland, Wales and Northern Ireland between 23 October and 15 November 2000. Interviews were conducted face to face at university sites.

Headline findings from the report show:

- By far the worst aspect of university life is having little money to spend and being in debt. On average, students currently owe and have to repay £3,326 as a result of attending university, and predict that they will owe, on average, £7,026 by the time they have completed their studies.
- Religion plays no part in almost half students' lives. However, 56% of students still believe in the institution of marriage.
- If there was to be a General Election tomorrow, Labour would win the largest proportion of the student vote with Conservatives and Liberal Democrats with just one percentage point between them for second place.
- One-fifth of students have been a victim of crime while at university.
- Only half of students plan to find a job in the UK once they have completed their current course.
- The majority of students have had some form of work experience during their time at university with 30% currently in a part-time job. Working part-time is more likely than not to have had an adverse affect on their university needs.
- 4% of students have a WAP phone, double the number who own a motorbike or motorised scooter. One-fifth (16%) spend their leisure time on the Internet and sending e-mails.
- Around half of university students currently live in private rented accommodation, one-fifth live in halls of residence, an identical proportion live with their parents or guardian and one in ten live in their own home.
- Two-fifths of students could not do one or more of the domestic activities specified such as cook, budget and iron before going to university.
- The majority of students do not view the Student Union as a political body but as a way of accessing the facilities and services they provide and obtaining discounted goods and services.
- Students continue to spend their spare time doing traditional 'student activities' such as going to the pub, meeting friends and watching TV. Two-fifths participate in sport, this is slightly higher among males (49%), females (38%).

Commenting on the *Student Living Report*, UNITE's Chief Executive, Nick Porter, said: 'Higher education students represent an important community as the future of the UK. Our survey is one of the most comprehensive studies of their views, concerns and aspirations. It will help universities and businesses to understand their requirements and ensure that, as real consumers of the education system, their needs are met.'

Professor Bob Worcester, Chairman of MORI, added: 'Today's students focus on gaining good qualifications to help them find the right job. While they are happy with their choice of university and recognise that university studies are a wise investment in their future, they are worried about their debts.'

Today, UNITE also unveils its unique student accommodation information and booking service – www.bunk.com which is set to revolutionise the sourcing and booking of accommodation for both universities, who are expected to save an average of £92,000, and for students who will save both time and expenses.

- Technical Note: MORI conducted 1,103 face-to-face interviews with full-time undergraduate and postgraduate students between 23 October and 15 November 2000.

© MORI (Market & Opinion Research International Limited)

Student debt trebles since end of grants

By Donald Macleod

Student debt has trebled to nearly £2,500 per year since grants were phased out, the Department for Education admitted today.

A study conducted by Claire Callender, professor of social policy at South Bank University, found that nearly nine out of 10 students complained of some financial difficulties, and six out of 10 believed these had harmed their academic work.

While the vast majority of students felt that their qualifications would help them get better jobs, one in 10 thought of dropping out of study because of lack of funding, while nearly two-thirds were convinced the funding system had deterred friends from going to university. This was most marked for those from poorer backgrounds, black students and women over 25. On average the amount students owed at the end of the academic year rose from £777 in 1995/96 to £2,473 in 1998/99 – equal to £7,584 over a three-year course.

Slipping the report out quietly just before Christmas, the Education and Employment minister Tessa Blackstone said that student income had grown in real terms over the three years. Most students received enough financial support to meet all their essential costs, she said.

'The survey evidence confirms that the great majority of full-time students are taking out new fairer income loans which are interest-free in real terms, with repayment linked to income. Students are generally receiving the support they need from loans, grants and contributions from their parents, but we recognise that further, targeted support is needed for some disadvantaged groups,' said Baroness Blackstone.

But the National Union of Students said the study was conducted when some maintenance grants were still available to the poorest students so the true position was even worse.

Owain James, NUS national president, said: 'The department's own survey is a damning indictment of the government's student funding system. Their figures show student hardship is widespread with 87% of students experiencing difficulty. What more evidence does the government need? The Scottish parliament has rejected their funding system. In England applications from poorer students have fallen. The government must act now to return maintenance grants to those from poorest backgrounds, as received by Scottish students.'

However the figures show that while students spent over £300 more on average on entertainment in 1999 than three years before, they were spending less on accommodation and food – possibly because more are living at home.

The proportion of students who failed to receive their full parental contribution doubled over the three years to three in 10 students. This left students to make up the outstanding amount of £719 calculated as a mean figure.

Among full-timers in the survey, student loan take-up was 72%. The most common reason given for not taking out a loan was that the student did not need the money. Other students preferred not to take out loans for personal or other reasons. There were no significant differences in take-up rates by gender or class, but among ethnic groups, Asian students had a relatively low take-up rate (51%).

• Meanwhile, vice-chancellors are launching their own study of student debt and attitudes towards funding, Universities UK announced today.

Diana Warwick, chief executive, said that heads of universities were taking these issues very seriously: 'Universities want their students to succeed and will be concerned about any evidence of debt which affects academic performance or causes hardship. They also want to reach out to new students, particularly those from poorer backgrounds who are currently not taking up higher education in sufficient numbers.

'If fear of debt is one of the factors deterring such applications – we will address this issue urgently as part of our current funding review.'

Student debt 'getting out of control'

**By Rebecca Smithers,
Education Correspondent**

Student debt is spiralling out of control, student leaders warned yesterday, as new government-funded research revealed that the vast majority of those on degree courses were in serious financial difficulties.

Not only were students borrowing more money than ever before from banks and credit card companies, the research showed, but prospective undergraduates were also being deterred from applying to university because of fears about being saddled with debt.

Opposition MPs claimed the findings proved the government's higher education policies – including the controversial introduction of tuition fees – were in disarray, and criticised ministers for putting a 'positive spin' on them.

The research into student finances is carried out by the Department for Education every three years, and was commissioned this time from Claire Callender of South Bank University and NOP Research.

The survey, based on personal interviews with 2,800 students on degree courses in the 1998-99 academic year, showed that student debts had trebled since 1995-96 when the last research took place. Nearly nine out of 10 students faced financial difficulties, while nearly two-thirds of respondents said a member of their peer group had opted not to go into higher education because of worries about debt.

In the three years of the study, between 1996 and 1999, student expenditure rose above the rate of inflation, fuelled by a 66% increase in money borrowed from banks and credit card companies, in addition to official student loans.

The average student debt was £2,473, compared with £777 three years earlier.

The research covered the 1998-99 academic year, a transitional period involving the first students affected by the Labour government's introduction of tuition fees.

Since 1995-96 younger students have experienced a drop of 30% in grant income and a fall of 17% in regular parental contributions.

Students are also supplementing their income by taking on more paid work, and using up more of their savings to fund their university education.

Owain James, president of the National Union of Students, warned: 'The DfEE's own survey is a damning indictment of the government's student funding system.'

He added: 'These figures show that student hardship is widespread.'

Higher education minister Tessa Blackstone said in a statement: 'The survey evidence confirms that the great majority of full-time students are taking our new fairer income loans, which are interest-free in real terms with repayment linked to income.'

Evan Harris, the Liberal Democrat higher education spokesman, said that the survey was a condemnation of the government's policy on students.

The shadow education secretary, Theresa May, said: 'No one should be deceived by this outrageous example of Labour spin.'

£5,100 to pay back and not enough money

Gemma Cantelo, 21, knows only too well the burden of debt facing graduates when they leave university. Gemma

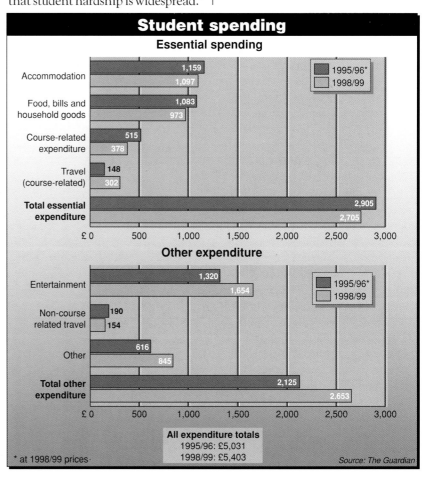

Student spending — Source: The Guardian

graduated last year and has a £3,100 student loan to pay off. She pays £10 a month interest on that money.

She also has a £2,000 overdraft which she ran up with her bank, as she had to borrow more money to live on during her three-year history and philosophy course at Cardiff University.

Because she earns less than £16,000 a year as a trainee librarian, she cannot afford to start paying off the loan until next year. She received a three-quarter grant from her local authority and her parents topped up the remaining quarter.

Gemma was determined to finish her course. One of her friends, a chemistry undergraduate dropped out of his course in the first year because he could not afford to continue. Another friend dropped out five years ago with the intention of returning after he had paid off his loan but so far has been unable to find the funds to return to his course.

Gemma gained an upper second and is keen to take a master's degree in information sciences but cannot afford to return to university.

She said: 'I think university was a worthwhile experience and my parents encouraged me to go as they are both graduates. But I think it is ridiculous that we are left facing this huge debt when we leave. I try not to think about how much I owe as it keeps me awake at night just worrying about how I am going to pay it off.

'I cannot borrow any more money because I am up to my overdraft limit. My parents are now having to find both grant money and tuition fees for my younger sister who is at university.

'With my starting salary there's little chance of me starting to pay off the loan at the moment and I am finding it quite tough affording rent in London.'

Gemma, from Canterbury, said that she managed to work during all her holidays but even this failed to make sufficient inroads into paying off the debt. Some of her friends had up to three term-time jobs, working as office cleaners or waitressing, which left precious little time for studying.

© Guardian Newspapers Limited 2000

Coping with debt

Information from the London School of Economics

Below is some general advice on how you might go about managing your debts. However, we strongly advise that you seek professional help with managing your money problems, especially if you feel the situation has got out of your control (e.g. if court action has been initiated). Your bank if they are student-friendly, or the Students' Union Advice Centre, should be your first port of call.

Tips for dealing with debtors

1. Prioritise your debts.

Ideally, you will be able to offer some monthly payment, however small, to all your creditors. But first of all, debts should be prioritised not on the basis of which are the largest, but based on the legal remedies open to creditors and the potential consequences of failing to pay certain debts. You should agree arrangements for paying all your priority debts first and then assess whether you are in a position to make offers to non-priority creditors.

Examples of priority debts include:

a. Debts such as council tax, fines, maintenance payable under a court order, compensation orders and tax – should be prioritised because court action or seizure of goods and even imprisonment are potential results of non-payment.

b. Rent arrears, loans secured on your home and utility charges (gas, electricity and water) are another group to be prioritised to prevent loss of your home or disconnection of supplies.

c. Debts to LSE itself may also be a priority for you since your exam results or degree may be withheld until payment is made.

d. Debts to relatives, friends or other students may also need to be prioritised if you are hoping to rely on those people for future support, or, for example, if your debt will lead to serious financial problems for the person who lent you money.

If you are having difficulty deciding which debts are priority debts or persuading a non-priority creditor that another debt should be treated as a priority then contact the Students' Union Advice Centre or a Citizens' Advice Bureau for advice.

2. Don't avoid contact with creditors.

Inform them of problems as early as possible and be honest. They are more likely to give you time to pay if you do this.

3. Don't avoid contact with your bank.

Banks are generally much friendlier if you approach them before you go over your authorised overdraft limit, and they begin to receive your bounced cheques. Remember they are the experts in money management, and some will even have special student advisers.

4. Keep copies of all correspondence.

This means everything from bank statements to the letters you send yourself. If you make contact by phone, ensure you obtain the name of the person you speak to and note the date of the call.

5. If you feel those you have contacted so far have been unsympathetic, write directly to the senior in charge of debt collection.

Remember that they are likely to be more sympathetic if a third party is involved (e.g. a welfare or bank adviser) since this demonstrates that you have been sensible enough to seek help.

6. If matters have already become serious, ask creditors to freeze interest at the point at which you make them a realistic offer of monthly payments.

7. Keep your promises.
Having drawn up a financial statement offering a certain amount every month, you must stick to it if possible! Creditors will lose any sympathy they might have had for you if you mess them about without good reason. If your circumstances have changed and you are no longer able to meet agreed payments you would need to explain this to your creditors, provide them with a new financial statement and ask them to agree to accept amended payments until your circumstances improve. If your circumstances have changed, remember to ensure that you have first made provision for paying priority debts.

8. Remember your rights.
A debtor cannot be sent to prison for non-payment except in the case of certain debts such as council tax, income tax, National Insurance, maintenance payable under a court order, child support and fines. Similarly, a debtor cannot be prosecuted in the Criminal Court (only in the County Court) except in the case of these and similar debts – seek advice if you are not sure. Having said that, County Court Judgments have serious implications; they can affect your credit rating for many years, and if you are sued for a debt you will not only have to pay the debt with interest, but will also be expected to pay substantial court

fees and costs. The company that sues you may also charge fees for their administration in issuing the original summons. All this means is that it makes even more sense to deal with your debts before things are taken this far.

Harassment is illegal no matter what you owe. Harassment is defined as attempting to coerce a person to pay a debt by making demands which subject a person to 'alarm, distress or humiliation, because of their frequency or publicity or manner' (Administration of Justice Act 1970, section 40). Harassment includes actions such as falsely claiming court proceedings may be instituted or have been instituted, or that property may legally be seized in lieu of payment without the permission of a court. Harassment also includes making nuisance visits or phone calls or using abusive or threatening language in correspondence or conversation. Credit card and mail order companies etc. will often send numerous threatening letters to try and make you pay them because they know that a court will not consider them a priority debt. Don't be intimidated into paying more than you can afford

Sorting out repayments
Here's one example of how you can begin to deal with your debts before things go too far. Again, this is best done with a welfare adviser, or a bank adviser to help.
1. Set a realistic budget for yourself, establishing how much you have available to pay creditors once you have allowed essential expenditure on food, travel and

rent etc. (if you drafted a budget at the beginning of the year, this should be easy).
2. Remember that certain 'ongoing' bills such as water, electricity and gas will need you to make sufficient payments to cover the charges you are still accumulating (i.e. the water, gas etc. you are still using) plus an amount towards the outstanding debt.
3. Contact all those you owe money to and find out exactly how much you owe in total.
4. After you have made arrangements to deal with your priority debts and have allowed for essential expenditure such as food, toiletries, travel costs and rent divide any remaining money you have available amongst your non-priority creditors on an equitable basis – this means working out each debt as a percentage of the total debt you owe to all your creditors. Then you should divide the amount of money you have available on the same percentage basis. For example, if your total debt was £200, and you owed one creditor £100, as a percentage that would be 50% of your £200 total. If you had £20 a month with which to repay your debts, you would offer 50% of that £20 to the creditor to whom you owed £100 – which would be £10 a month.
5. Draw up a financial statement that details all the figures you have worked out above: show income and essential expenditure, highlight exactly how much you have left for repayment of

non-priority debts every month, and finally list the total you owe to each creditor and the amount you are offering to pay each month on the basis of equitable distribution.

6. This process may take some time, but it will allow you to demonstrate to each creditor that you are making them a realistic offer. Remember that a small but regular payment is better than none at all.

7. Send a copy of your financial statement to each creditor with a covering letter explaining the difficulties you have been experiencing, asking for interest to be frozen henceforth on the basis of the monthly payments offered in your financial statement. Ask the creditor to send you a paying-in book or standing order form. Finally, advise your creditors that you will keep them informed of any

changes in your circumstances. You could point out that you will make an improved offer in the event that your financial circumstances improve if you think this is likely to happen.

8. Keep copies of all correspondence with your creditors, and make notes of phone calls detailing the date and the name of the person you spoke to.

© London School of Economics & Political Science Students' Union

Managing your money

Information from the National Union of Students (NUS)

More and more opportunities for debt and credit are offered to students (for example, through loans, overdrafts and credit cards), so it is imperative that students are aware of the pitfalls as well as the advantages and temptations of various sources of income. Mismanaging debt may have serious implications legally as well as financially. This information offers some tips for managing your money and managing debt.

Money management support

Many college student services and/or students' union welfare services offer money management and debt counselling services. NUS would advise prospective and existing students to make use of these services early in their course to boost money management skills.

Budgeting
Work out what income you have and what you will have to spend, for example each month. The institution should have student advisers in the students' union and the college who can help with this. This will help you to work out if you need more money. You may want to complete a budget planner such as the one below.

Record keeping
Make sure you keep up-to-date records of your income, spending and sources of debt. Your college or students' union may be able to help you to set up records and monitor your records.

Understand your entitlements
Make sure you know what funding you are entitled to and what else you may be able to apply for in terms of student support, for example Access Funds and other college funds, or charitable sources. Make sure you make the most of discounts available to you, such as through the NUS Card.

Coping with debt
If you find that you are not managing your finances, but your finances are managing you – seek advice from your institution, your students'

union, or your local Citizens' Advice Bureau. They may help you with prioritising your debts, corresponding with creditors and managing a budget.

Banking

Banks tend to offer specific preferential services to full-time undergraduates. Students on courses of further education and postgraduate education may find it more difficult to secure preferential services, such as interest-free overdrafts or higher rate cheque guarantee cards. How-

Monthly budget planner			
INCOME	£	**Variable outgoings**	£
Student loan		Travel costs	
Grant		Books/stationery/photocopying	
Contribution from family		Telephone calls	
Earnings		Food/meals	
Other		Laundry	
Total		Clothing	
		Toiletries	
MONTHLY EXPENDITURE		Sports/hobbies/leisure	
Fixed outgoings		Club/society subscriptions	
Rent/mortgage		Occasional costs (e.g.	
Gas/electricity		holidays. presents etc.)	
Telephone (rental)		Other	
Water rates		**Total:**	....
Insurance			
TV licence/rental		**Total monthly expenditure**	....
Other			
Total	....		

MONTHLY BUDGET	**£**	
Monthly income	....	
Minus total outgoings	....	
TOTAL MONTHLY BUDGET	....	

ever, a few banks are catching onto this, particularly within the 16-19 age range. Important points to stress are:

- Shop around for the best offer for you (e.g. some students may want £35 as an incentive for opening an account whereas others may prefer retail discounts).
- Check the availability of the branches near your intended place of study and whether the bank has a specific Student Officer available. Having a face-to-face staff officer who understands the needs of students often helps when you are facing particular problems – e.g. your grant/loan cheque hasn't arrived on time.
- Try to open a bank account before starting college – you will avoid the crush and save time in getting access to the services and to your money.

N.B. Many banks now offer graduate accounts which offer graduating students a period of interest-free overdraft or a preferential rate on loans. Make sure that you check the conditions linked to these accounts, for example, what is the maximum interest-free overdraft offered? What will happen to your outstanding overdraft? When will the interest free period end, and what happens then? Can you merge a number of debts?

Sources of income

Paid work

The NUS Student Hardship Survey (1999) found that 41% of full-time undergraduates sampled worked during periods of study. The average hours of work were 13 per week and average pay was £4.53 per hour. If you are considering working whilst studying, it is worth thinking about your options – e.g. does the college/students' union run an employment agency (this way, you may be guaranteed at least the minimum wage)? What is the average wage for your area? What type of work is available in your area (i.e. shift work, evenings, weekends)? What hours will fit into your pattern of studies? Is there union representation within the workplace to protect your health and safety and employment rights?

Using credit

If you are using credit – e.g. a credit card, store card, buying from a catalogue – check the interest rates and repayment conditions. Commercial lending often incurs severe penalties if borrowers don't keep to the repayment terms, so make sure you know what you are getting yourself into and try to use these sources as a last resort. If you are using credit, keep an eye on what you are using such credit for, e.g. if you are using your credit card to pay for your food then it is likely that you need to seek financial advice and/or additional financial support from your institution.

Sources of expenditure

Course costs

'Hidden' course costs – i.e. those costs not covered by upfront tuition fees – are an increasing cost for students. Find out how much a course is likely to actually cost per year. Information should be available either within an institution's prospectus, from the course tutor or possibly from the students' union. Important points include: Are you required to buy a lot of equipment (e.g. Arts and Textiles, Engineering, Architecture courses)? What books will you need? Are you required to photocopy study packs/books and how much will this cost per term? Will you be required to attend field trips and how much will this cost per term? Then think about how you can save on these costs – Can you share books/equipment with other students? Can the institution help with costs of equipment and books through the Access/Hardship Funds?

Living costs

Find out the average costs for living near the college (your students' union or institution may provide estimates). This will help you decide whether you can afford an area with the money you expect to have.

- The above information is an extract from Information Sheet 17 – *Managing your Money*, produced by the National Union of Students' Welfare Unit.

Loans

Information from studentUK

Loans, loans everywhere . . . but not a drop to spend on drink. Loans are now fully integrated in the student mind. They are a necessity after the abolition of the grant system. And every year the system changes slightly. This year, 75% of the maximum loan entitlement does NOT depend on your family's income, whereas before the entire loan didn't. The loans are payable in three instalments at the beginning of each term. The amounts you could receive are:

	Full Year	75%	Final Year	75%
London	£4,590	£3,445	£3,980	£2,985
Elsewhere	£3,725	£2,795	£3,230	£2,425
Home	£2,950	£2,215	£2,575	£1,935

You have to be under 55 to qualify for a loan.

Repaying the loan

You'll start repaying your loan in the April after you finish or leave your course. If you are earning over £10,000, 9% of your income will be taken. If you are earning less than that, you won't have to pay anything until you do. The repayments will be collected from your pay via the Inland Revenue.

Income	Earnings Repayment per month
£10,000	Nil
£15,000	£37
£20,000	£75

ADDITIONAL RESOURCES

You might like to contact the following organisations for further information. Due to the increasing cost of postage, many organisations cannot respond to enquiries unless they receive a stamped, addressed envelope.

Centre for Policy Studies
57 Tufton Street
London
SW1P 3QL
Tel: 020 7222 4488
Fax: 020 7222 4388
Web site: www.cps.org.uk
The Centre for Policy Studies (CPS) is an independent centre-right think tank which develops and publishes public policy proposals and arranges seminars and lectures on topical policy issues, as part of its mission to influence policy around the world. It also maintains a range of informal contacts with politicians, policymakers, civil servants and the press, in Britain and abroad.

Department for Education and Employment (DfEE)
Public Enquiry Unit
Castle View House
East Lane
Runcorn
Cheshire
WA7 2GU
Tel: 0870 000 2288
Fax: 01928 794248
E-mail: info@dfee.gov.uk
Web site: www.dfee.gov.uk
The Department for Education and Employment is the UK Government department with the overall aim 'to give everyone the chance, through education, training and work, to realise their full potential, and thus build an inclusive and fair society and a competitive economy'.

London School of Economics
Houghton Street
London
WC2A 2AE
Tel: 020 7405 7686
Fax: 020 7955 7733
Web site: www.lse.ac.uk
The London School of Economics and Political Science (LSE) is unique in the United Kingdom in its concentration on teaching and research across the full range of the social, political and economic sciences.

National Audit Office
157-197 Buckingham Palace Road
London
SW1W 9SP
Tel: 020 7798 7000
Fax: 020 7828 3774
E-mail: enquiries@nao.gsi.gov.uk
Web site: www.nao.gov.uk
For general enquiries about the work of the National Audit Office or more general information please contact: The Information Centre Helpdesk: Telephone 020 7798 7264. Fax 020 7798 7894.

National Union of Teachers
Hamilton House
Mabledon Place
London
WC1H 9BD
Tel: 020 7388 6191
Fax: 020 7387 8458
Web site: www.teachers.org.uk
The NUT is the largest and most influential teachers' organisation.

studentUK
5 Baden Place
Crosby Row
London
SE1 1YW
Tel: 020 7407 0186
Fax: 020 7407 1176
Web site: www.studentuk.com
studentUK owes its very existence to the Nottinghamshire-based publishing company W&J Linney Ltd and UCAS. They have given us their efforts and most importantly the resources to create what they think is THE best student site on the web.

The Office for Standards in Education (OFSTED)
Alexandra House
33 Kingsway
London
WC2B 6SE
Tel: 020 7421 6800
Web site: www.ofsted.gov.uk
The Office for Standards in Education (OFSTED) is the Office of Her Majesty's Chief Inspector of Schools in England.

INDEX

★★★★★

The Internet has been likened to shopping in a supermarket without aisles. The press of a button on a Web browser can bring up thousands of sites but working your way through them to find what you want can involve long and frustrating on-line searches.

And unfortunately many sites contain inaccurate, misleading or heavily biased information. Our researchers have therefore undertaken an extensive analysis to bring you a selection of quality Web site addresses.

National Union of Teachers (NUT)
www.teachers.org.uk
The National Union of Teachers web site gives information on issues affecting educators. Click on Key Policies for more detailed information.

National Union of Students (NUS)
www.nusonline.co.uk
A very useful site with lots of information on education issues.

Department for Education and Employment (DfEE)
www.dfee.gov.uk
A government web site with a large amount of information on educational issues.

The Office for Standards in Education (OFSTED)
www.ofsted.gov.uk
An easy to use web site with inspection reports, press releases and publications available to view.

Centre for Policy Studies
www.cps.org.uk
This web site lists their education pamphlets with brief summaries which can be purchased.

studentUK
www.studentuk.com
Studentuk web site gives advice and information on a wide range of topics.

ACKNOWLEDGEMENTS

The publisher is grateful for permission to reproduce the following material.

While every care has been taken to trace and acknowledge copyright, the publisher tenders its apology for any accidental infringement or where copyright has proved untraceable. The publisher would be pleased to come to a suitable arrangement in any such case with the rightful owner.

Chapter One: Educational Standards

The National Curriculum, © Qualifications and Curriculum Authority (QCA) , *Educational outcomes*, © European Commission/EUROSTAT, *Jargon-busting guide*, © Crown copyright is reproduced with the permission of the Controller of Her Majesty's Stationery Office, *Britain bottom of literacy league*, © Telegraph Group Limited, London 2000, *Tests show pupils have better grasp of basics*, © Telegraph Group Limited, London 2000, *The greater divide*, © Guardian Newspapers Limited 2001, *Bridging the gender gap*, © Guardian Newspapers Limited 2001, *Pupils achieving 5 or more GCSE grades A*-C*, © Crown copyright is reproduced with the permission of the Controller of Her Majesty's Stationery Office, *How exams are fixed in favour of girls*, © 2001 The Spectator, *Educational inequality*, © Crown copyright is reproduced with the permission of the Controller of Her Majesty's Stationery Office, *GCSE attainment by ethnicity*, © Crown copyright is reproduced with the permission of the Controller of Her Majesty's Stationery Office, *Black pupils three times more likely to be barred*, © Telegraph Group Limited, London 2000, *Worsening behaviour 'linked to teacher shortage'*, © Guardian Newspapers Limited 2001, *Truancy checks in city centre cut youth crime*, © Telegraph Group Limited, London 2001, *Teacher shortages threaten standards*, © Telegraph Group Limited, London 2000, *NUT tells Government how to end teacher shortage crisis*, © The National Union of Teachers (NUT), *Britain has the worst schools in Europe*, © The Daily Mail, March 2001, *Improving student performance*, © UK National Audit Office, *The betrayed generations*, © Centre for Policy Studies, *Student drop outs cost £200m a year*, © Guardian Newspapers Limited 2001, *Universities and colleges*, © Organisation for Economic Co-operation and Development (OECD), *Bread but no honey*, © Guardian Newspapers Limited 2001, *Fair deal?*, © Guardian Newspapers Limited 2001, *Building for the future*, © Crown copyright is reproduced with the permission of the Controller of Her Majesty's Stationery Office.

Chapter Two: The Cost of an Education

The student of 2000: more work, less play, © Telegraph Group Limited, London 2001, *Student earners lose out twice*, © Guardian Newspapers Limited 2001, *Frequently asked questions*, © Crown copyright is reproduced with the permission of the Controller of Her Majesty's Stationery Office, *Students being excluded*, © Guardian Newspapers Limited 2001, *Students living in Scotland*, © Crown copyright is reproduced with the permission of the Controller of Her Majesty's Stationery Office, *Students learn a hard lesson about debt*, © Telegraph Group Limited, London 2000, *Work*, © studentUK 2001, *Student living report*, © MORI (Market & Opinion Research International Limited), *Student debt trebles since end of grants*, © Guardian Newspapers Limited 2001, *Student debt 'getting out of control'*, © Guardian Newspapers Limited 2001, *Student spending*, © Guardian Newspapers Limited 2001, *Coping with debt*, © London School of Economics & Political Science Students' Union, *Managing your money*, © National Union of Students (NUS), *Monthly budget planner*, © National Union of Students (NUS), *Loans*, student UK 2001.

Photographs and illustrations:

Pages 1, 16, 25, 30: Pumpkin House, pages 4, 6, 14,18, 22, 26, 28, 38: Simon Kneebone, page 35: Michaela Bloomfield.

Craig Donnellan
Cambridge
April, 2001